Second Edition

Advertising & Marketing Checklists

Second Edition

Advertising & Marketing Checklists

107 PROVEN CHECKLISTS TO SAVE TIME & BOOST ADVERTISING & MARKETING EFFECTIVENESS

Ron Kaatz

NTC Business Books
a division of *NTC Publishing Group* • Lincolnwood, Illinois USA

Library of Congress Cataloging-in-Publication Data

Kaatz, Ronald B.
　　Advertising & marketing checklists: 107 proven checklists to save time
　& boost advertising & marketing effectiveness / Ron Kaatz.—2nd ed.

　　　p. cm.
　　ISBN 0–8442-3520-2
　　1. Advertising—Handbooks, manuals, etc.　I. Title.　II. Title:
　Advertising and marketing checklists.
HF5823.K22 1995　　　　　　　　　　　　　　　　　94-14171
659.1–dc20　　　　　　　　　　　　　　　　　　　　　CIP

1995 Printing

Published by NTC Business Books, a division of NTC Publishing Group.
©1995, 1989 by NTC Publishing Group, 4255 West Touhy Avenue,
Lincolnwood (Chicago), Illinois 60646-1975. U.S.A.
Manufactured in the United States of America.
Library of Congress Catalog Card No. 94-14171

5 6 7 8 9 ML 9 8 7 6 5 4 3 2

With all my love to Suzi.

"The best advertising reference book just got better! The many new charts and checklists are like a speed course on new media and integrated communications.

If you just think of this book as 107 useful charts and checklists, that's reason enough for every marketer to have it on his or her bookshelf. But before you put it there, be sure to look through it. You're guaranteed to get a few *use-now* ideas."

Jim Kobs, *Chairman*
Kobs Gregory Passavant

"In an advertising world that demands versatility and customization from the modern agency, Ron Kaatz has given us a comprehensive guide to all facets of the advertising process. I recommend Ron's checklists to everyone in the business."

Keith Reinhard, *Chairman & CEO*
DDB Needham Worldwide

"Ron's first book offering 77 proven checklists has been a valuable reference source for advertising practitioners since 1989. Now we have 30 additional reasons to use the second edition."

David K. Braun, *Vice President, Media Services*
Kraft General Foods, Inc.

"No one is more aware of how change will affect our marketing and advertising concepts than Ron Kaatz. In his new book, Ron continues to simplify the most complex advertising and marketing concepts and leads you, step-by-step, through the basic fundamentals as well as the present and future changes that are taking place in the world of marketing."

Alvin M. Eicoff, *Chairman*
A. Eicoff & Co.

"Ron Kaatz has been on the firing line and understands the realities of the advertising and marketing business. His book is a must-read for those in the trenches.

In a business where change is a daily reality, Ron Kaatz' book is an anchor for those who must make the day-to-day decisions."

Jack Myers, *President*
Myers Communications

"If you simply glance at Ron Kaatz' checklists at the start of each communications project, you'll almost certainly do a better job. If you actually answer the questions and address the issues, your probability of success will increase dramatically."

Burt Manning, *Chairman & CEO*
J. Walter Thompson Co.

"*Advertising & Marketing Checklists* is an indispensable reference book for every marketing professional today—thought-provoking, comprehensive, efficient, and practical."

Norman M. Goldring, *Chairman*
CPM Inc.

"This book may be so good for you that you'll need at least *two* copies—one to keep on the shelf for ready reference and another copy to mark up, tear apart, and carry with you to meetings."

Rance Crain, *President & Editorial Director*
Advertising Age

"As a practitioner, Ron Kaatz was a fine teacher. As a professor, he is still a fine practitioner. His lifelong collection of checklists will help everyone deal with the *why, what* and *how* of advertising."

Stephen A. Greyser, *Professor, Graduate School of Business Administration*
Harvard University

"Ron Kaatz' book is right on the money! I wish our clients would read it and use it when allocating their advertising and promotional funds."

Wayne LoCurto, *President & CEO*
ACTMEDIA

"*Advertising & Marketing Checklists* presents 30 years of experience in a unique manner that can be used easily by today's marketing professionals."

Gian Fulgoni, *Chairman & CEO*
Information Resources Inc.

"Kaatz has given us a reference which reminds experts of their discipline and allows general management to ask solid questions and participate in the marketing process. I believe it will prove to be of lasting value and a permanent addition to the literature."

Miles K. Marsh, *Chairman & CEO*
Pet Incorporated

"It's all here—from the basics to today's hottest topics, from coming up with winning ideas to the latest thinking on interactivity, new information delivery systems, and integrated marketing communications. Kaatz serves up the marketing wisdom of the ages, ingeniously, in an easy-to-apply and ready-to-use format.

Thomas L. Harris, *Managing Partner*
Thomas L. Harris & Co.

"I know a world champion when I meet one—and Ron Kaatz is a winner. If you want to hit more home runs and cut down on the strikeouts, buy a copy of the second edition of *Advertising & Marketing Checklists* today."

Charles O. Finley, *Former Owner, Oakland Athletics*
Charles O. Finley & Company, Inc.

Table of Contents

Foreword   xiii
Introduction   xv

Part I
The Basics: Why Do We Advertise? How Do We Get Ideas?   1
  1. 33 Reasons to Advertise   2
  2. 7 Key Reasons to Protect Your Brands   4
  3. The 13-Point Marketing Communications Needs Assessor   6
  4. A 9-Point Integrated Marketing Communications Checkup   8
  5. The Ben Franklin Advertising Option Evaluator   10
  6. The Advertising Effectiveness Idea Provoker   11
  7. Coming Up with a New Idea: Part I   12
  8. Coming Up with a New Idea: Part II   13
  9. Coming Up with a New Idea: Part III   14
 10. Developing New Ideas in a Group: 11 Reminders   16
 11. Marketing a New Product? A 15-Point Early Warning System   17

Part II
Creating the Messages   18
 12. The Communications Strategy Statement Planning Worksheet   19
 13. Consumer Benefit Evaluator   21
 14. 31 Ways in Which Advertising Appeals to the Consumer   22
 15. 35 Ways in Which Advertising Gets Attention & Communicates   24
 16. A Road Map for Moving from an Idea to a Message That Sells   26
 17. Good Ads & Bad Ads: 9 Characteristics   28
 18. 9 Tips for Creating More Effective Print Ads   29
 19. How to Avoid the Most Common Mistakes in Writing Copy   31
 20. 10 Keys to Effective Yellow Pages Advertising   32
 21. 12 Guidelines to Effective Outdoor Signage   34
 22. 6 Simple Tips for In-Store Customer Contacts   36
 23. Guidelines for Creating TV Commercials That Sell   37
 24. A Last-Minute Checkup on Your TV Storyboard   40
 25. The 14 Key Values of Infomercials   43
 26. Guidelines for Creating Radio Commercials That Sell   46

Contents

27. The Local Advertising Idea-Starter Kit   49
28. Should You Sponsor a Video?   59

Part III

Maneuvering through the Media   60

29. Sound Media Management: 10 Principles   61
30. A Model for Media Planning   63
31. The Preplanning Process   65
32. Checking Up on Your Media Plan   67
33. Monitoring Your Agency's Media Capabilities   69
34. 107 Customer Contact Points from A to Z   72
35. The Media Value Checklist   77
36. 20 Points for Assessing the Value of Place-Based Media   85
37. Implementing a Media Buy   88
38. 35 Value-Added Media Opportunities   89
39. Guiding the Search for a Creative Media Concept   91
40. The Creative Media Pocket Planner   94
41. How to Evaluate TV Special Sponsorship Opportunities   97
42. Questions to Ask When Considering Sponsorship of an Event   100
43. How to Evaluate a New Media Opportunity   104
44. 11 Keys to the Success of a New Information Delivery System   105
45. Two-Way Interactivity: 11 Insights   106
46. Reaching Customers in a High-Tech Environment:
       12 Facts of Life   108
47. A Guide to 19 Key Media Terms   109
48. Customer Contact Reach Calculator   113

Part IV

Public Relations, Publicity, and Promotions   114

49. 20 Public Relations, Publicity, and Promotional Ideas   115
50. A 17-Point Press Release Checklist   122
51. 6 Guidelines for Responding to a Threatened Boycott   124

Part V

Targeting and Selling through Direct Marketing   125

52. When to Use Direct Marketing   126
53. Bob Stone's Tips for Direct Marketing Success (Abridged)   129
54. A Guide to Profitable & Productive Business-to-Business
       Telemarketing   134

Contents

55. Guidelines to Effective Frequency-Marketing Programs 137
56. A Final Checkup for Effective Catalog Copy 139
57. Art or Photography in Catalogs: Which Way Should You Go? 141
58. 11 Keys to Home Shopping Success 142
59. 12 Keys to the Effective Use of Direct Marketing Order Forms 143

Part VI
Maximizing the Sales Promotion Payoff 145

60. The Do's and Cannot Do's of Consumer Sales Promotion 146
61. Consumer Sales Promotion: 41 Idea Starters 148
62. The Do's and Cannot Do's of Trade Sales Promotion 151
63. Promotion Planning Checklist 152
64. "Never-to-Be-Forgotten" Rules for Contests and Sweepstakes 157
65. Grocery Cross-Promotions: 120 Idea Starters 159

Part VII
Researching Your Marketing Communications Activities' Health and Well-Being 161

66. 16 Ways to Gather Consumer Insights 162
67. 10 Steps to Better Decisions 165
68. The 14-Point Advertising Response Monitor 167
69. An 18-Point Checkup on the Use of Research Reports 170
70. 11 Questions to Ask When Hiring a Research Company 173
71. 7 Fresh Ideas for a Simple, Homegrown Research Project 175
72. The Retailer's Advertising Impact Scorecard 177
73. How Much Frequency Is Enough? 178
74. Guidelines to Special Target Markets 180
75. Working with Numbers & Tables: 14 Tips 182

Part VIII
Communicating to Win 185

76. 14 Tips to a Winning Presentation 186
77. 6 Steps to Learning from Failure 188
78. 10 Guidelines to Communicating across Cultures 189
79. Guidelines for Using Numbers in Presentations 190
80. The "Never-to-Be-Forgotten" Pocket Presentation Planner 191
81. Negotiating to Win: 9 Tips 194
82. Winning at New Business: 11 Guidelines 196
83. 30 Ways for an Agency to Establish Good Client Relations 199

Contents

84. When Should You Put It in Writing? 201
85. More Effective Business Writing: A 3-Step Approach 202
86. Writing for Information: A 7-Step Approach 203
87. Writing an Effective Sales Letter: A 4-Step Checklist 204
88. 7 Tips for More Productive Meetings 207
89. Conferences and Special Events: A 151-Item Checklist 208
90. 6 Tips for Efficient Filing 212

Part IX
The Job, Money, and Travel Survival Kit 213
91. The Job Hunting Action Planner 214
92. The Resume Planning Form 215
93. 11 Questions to Ask Yourself about a Prospective Employee 217
94. The Marketing Communicator's Income Tax Saver 219
95. The Not-to-Be-Forgotten Business Traveler's Checklist 221
96. Fitness on the Move 222
97. The Business Traveler's Basic Health Kit 223
98. 12 Tips to Keep Long-Distance Travel from Becoming Travail 224

Part X
The Tool Kit 225
99. Decisions and Actions 226
100. Working Calendar 227
101. Planning Ledger 228
102. Strategic Plotter 229
103. Flow Chart 230
104. Media Spending Analyzer 231
105. Customer Contact Planner 232
106. U.S. Market Planner 234
107. The Multi-Factor Marketing Wheel 240

Foreword

When Ron Kaatz first told me about his plans for the second edition of *Advertising & Marketing Checklists*, I knew it would be a winner.

Since the first edition was published in 1989, thousands of marketing decision-makers have used it to make faster, smarter and more profitable decisions every time they picked it up.

Ron delivered *exactly* what he had promised.

And this second edition offers even more—about 40% more, if you're counting.

I've been a marketing communicator for over 40 years. Never have I seen so much change as is taking place today with the consumer, with the message delivery systems to reach the consumer, and in the marketplace.

Ron prepares you to deal with *all* of this. He has carefully reviewed and updated his original 77 checklists and charts—and has expertly crafted 30 new checklists that you will need to compete successfully in the competitive marketing environment of the 1990s and beyond.

If you invested in the first edition of *Advertising & Marketing Checklists*, you know that Ron wastes neither his words nor your time. In this second edition, he proves this again by quickly showing you how to deal comfortably with all of those critical new issues that are changing the ways in which you must work and think today and tomorrow. I'm talking about integrated marketing communications, two-way interactivity, infomercials, home shopping, value-added programs, place-based media, frequency marketing, telemarketing, cross-promotions and communications across cultures. And that's just for starters!

Advertising & Marketing Checklists is a "survival kit." And, fortunately, Ron is the perfect person to help you survive. In 30 years at Leo Burnett Co., CBS and J. Walter Thompson, Ron's associates could always count on him to produce a fast and effective solution to a problem. Today, the Integrated Marketing Communications Department of Northwestern's Medill School of Journalism is fortunate to benefit from his superb teaching.

In today's highly competitive environment, whether you are faced with the simplest or the most complex problem, you need all the help you can get to survive. This second edition of *Advertising & Marketing Checklists* will help you to not only survive, but to prosper. Put it to work for you today.

> **Richard C. Christian,** *Associate Dean*
> Medill School of Journalism, Northwestern University
> Founder and Past Chairman, Marsteller, Inc.
> (Marsteller Advertising & Burson-Marsteller Public Relations)
>
> Inductee, Advertising Hall of Fame

Introduction

Since the first edition of *Advertising & Marketing Checklists* was published in 1989, hardly a week has gone by that there hasn't been at least one announcement of changes. Changes in the consumer. Changes in the marketplace. And changes in the communications options to reach this consumer.

In this environment, the job of the marketer has become far more complex than it once was. Business-as-usual means *no* business to companies who must deal with:

- a consumer who has become a tougher customer,

- a consumer who is more and more promotion-driven,

- a consumer who expresses doubts and fears about the future,

- a consumer who is looking for someone or something to trust,

- a consumer who is barraged by claims and counterclaims, and

- a consumer who lives in a world of growing media fragmentation.

To survive and prosper in this environment, a company must make more critical decisions about more issues affecting more people and more dollars than ever before—all in *less* time! That is what this second edition of *Advertising & Marketing Checklists* will help you do.

To reflect the many changes that have taken place since 1989, this edition has been fully updated and expanded from 77 to 107 checklists and charts. Each and every one of them will save you time and boost your marketing communications' effectiveness.

You will profit from new checklists focusing on integrated marketing communications, two-way interactivity, infomercials, home shopping, value-added programs, place-based media, frequency marketing, telemarketing and cross-promotions. There are also new checklsts to guide you in a "preplanning" process, in monitoring your agency's media capabilities, in evaluating new information delivery systems, in gathering consumer insights and delivering customer contacts, and in communicating across cultures.

My goal has been to enable you to work smarter, faster, and easier. This second edition of *Advertising & Marketing Checklists* retains the same simple-to-follow structure that made the first edition so successful. Its many tools will help you assess your marketing communications needs, get new ideas and create the messages to contact your customers; maneuver through the media; handle public relations, direct marketing, sales promotion and research; prepare effective presentations; and successfully write and negotiate.

Advertising & Marketing Checklists is for every marketing communicator. It is for the multinational corporation with a $500 million marketing communications budget and the suburban store that spends $5,000 in a local newspaper.

Most importantly, it is not meant just to be read and put on the shelf. *Advertising & Marketing Checklists* is an interactive problem-solver. It is to be taken apart, copied, filled in, and added to. Where there are questions to answer, answer them. Where there are spaces to be filled in with your ideas and thoughts, fill them in. Probe your thinking so that you understand your responses. Take *Advertising & Marketing Checklists* into meetings with you, and carry sections in your pocket or briefcase. Use the book in whatever ways work best for *you*.

Introduction

I had even more fun writing this second edition of *Advertising & Marketing Checklists* than I did with the first edition. I want you to have fun using it. Since it is interactive, please write me with your thoughts, questions and suggestions for future checklists and charts.

Enjoy!

Part I

The Basics:
Why Do We Advertise?
How Do We Get Ideas?

Whether you are General Motors Corporation or a Chevrolet dealership in Sioux Falls, South Dakota...Procter & Gamble Co. or Sunset Foods in Highland Park, Illinois ...John Hancock Life Insurance Co. or The McRae Insurance Agency in Winston-Salem, North Carolina, you have asked yourself these questions more than once. These 11 checklists and charts all focus on the basics: how you might benefit from advertising, how you can assess your total marketing communications needs, and how you can come up with fresh, new ideas to accomplish these needs and make your business grow.

1. 33 Reasons to Advertise
2. 7 Key Reasons to Protect Your Brands
3. The 13-Point Marketing Communications Needs Assessor
4. A 9-Point Integrated Marketing Communications Checkup
5. The Ben Franklin Advertising Option Evaluator
6. The Advertising Effectiveness Idea Provoker
7. Coming Up with a New Idea: Part I
8. Coming Up with a New Idea: Part II
9. Coming Up with a New Idea: Part III
10. Developing New Ideas in a Group: 11 Reminders
11. Marketing a New Product? A 15-Point Early Warning System

33 Reasons to Advertise

One of the most frequently asked questions by everyone who is concerned about the cost of doing business is "Why should I advertise?" In the first column, check off all those reasons why you believe *your competition* advertises. In the second column, check off every reason why *your business* might benefit from advertising. Your responses will not only help provide you with a rationale for advertising, but they will also point to new directions that your advertising or perhaps your other marketing communications activities should take.

	Why Does Competition Advertise?	Why Should We Advertise?
1. To attract new customers	☐	☐
2. To increase the frequency of use	☐	☐
3. To increase the number of different uses	☐	☐
4. To increase the number of different users	☐	☐
5. To increase the quantity purchased	☐	☐
6. To increase the frequency of replacement	☐	☐
7. To increase the length of the buying season	☐	☐
8. To switch customers from other companies or brands	☐	☐
9. To bring a family of brands together	☐	☐
10. To turn a disadvantage into an advantage	☐	☐
11. To attract a new generation of users	☐	☐
12. To create, enhance, or maintain image, prestige, or leadership	☐	☐
13. To introduce something new	☐	☐
14. To reintroduce something old	☐	☐

33 Reasons to Advertise

	Why Does Competition Advertise?	Why Should We Advertise?
15. To introduce or announce a new company	☐	☐
16. To support a promotion	☐	☐
17. To promote an entire industry	☐	☐
18. To open doors for the sales force	☐	☐
19. To introduce a new company name	☐	☐
20. To reposition a company	☐	☐
21. To rise above the competition	☐	☐
22. To gain professional approval or endorsement	☐	☐
23. To maintain professional approval or endorsement	☐	☐
24. To improve employee morale	☐	☐
25. To boost sales force productivity	☐	☐
26. To develop sales leads	☐	☐
27. To conduct research	☐	☐
28. To enter new markets	☐	☐
29. To offer brochures and reports	☐	☐
30. To support a cause	☐	☐
31. To oppose a cause	☐	☐
32. To combat unfavorable publicity	☐	☐
33. To announce something fast	☐	☐

7 Key Reasons to Protect Your Brands

Brands are a company's most precious assets. However, they require constant care and feeding. To grow and prosper, a company must create, sustain, protect, enhance, and leverage its brands. One of the greatest mistakes a company can make is to cut its brand marketing efforts during weak economic times. The result can be a costly loss of brand share that is very difficult to make up later. How do the following seven key brand assets apply to you? Why is it important for you to protect your brands?

1. Brands save my customers time and simplify their product purchase process.

   It is very important for me to protect this because _____

   _____ .

2. Brands send a message to my customers that they can trust my product and that they can depend on its consistency.

   It is very important for me to protect this because _____

   _____ .

3. Brands can define who my customers are. (For example, beer drinkers wear their brand as a badge. "I'm a Bud drinker!")

   It is very important for me to protect this because _____

   _____ .

4. A top brand can command a top price.

   It is very important for me to protect this because _____

   _____ .

5. A successful brand can permit line extensions. This is very important because it is far less costly for me to develop line extensions than to introduce totally new products.

   It is very important for me to protect this because _____

   _____ .

6. Brands provide leverage for me with the trade when it comes to shelf space, promotions, etc.

It is very important for me to protect this because _____

_____ .

7. Brands can increase the value of my company's stock.

It is very important for me to protect this because _____

_____ .

The 13-Point Marketing Communications Needs Assessor

Every business must continually reassess its performance. This includes an appraisal of the degree to which its overall marketing communications efforts accomplish its agreed-upon objectives. *The 13-Point Marketing Communications Needs Assessor* helps you conduct your appraisal.

1. What are the goals of your business?

    _____

    _____

2. To what degree have these goals been met?

    _____

    _____

3. Overall, what are your business's greatest strengths?

    _____

    _____

4. What have been your major problem areas?

    _____

    _____

5. If you had to do it all over again, what would you do differently?

    _____

    _____

6. Where do most of your present customers come from?

    _____

    _____

7. What customers that you do not now serve would you like to have?

_____

_____

8. What form have your past marketing communications activities taken?

_____

_____

9. How much have you allocated to spend on your marketing communications activities in the past?

_____

_____

10. What are your priorities for the next 12 months in terms of the growth of your business?

_____

_____

11. What objectives do you want your marketing communications activities to accomplish?

_____

_____

12. How much will it cost you to accomplish these objectives?

_____

_____

13. How will you know if your marketing communications activities succeed in meeting these objectives?

_____

_____

A 9-Point Integrated Marketing Communications Checkup

Where do you stand on developing an Integrated Marketing Communications (IMC) program for your business? Whether you sell a consumer product or a service to industry, ask yourself each of these nine questions. Where your answer is "No," write down what you might do to accomplish this.

	YES	NO

1. Do you really understand your customers and your prospective customers? Have you gathered all of the information on them that will guide you in planning? ☐ ☐

This can be accomplished by _____

_____ .

2. Does everyone in your company who can contribute to the development of an effective IMC program participate in the process? ☐ ☐

This can be accomplished by _____

_____ .

3. Do all of your outside agencies who can contribute to the development of an effective IMC program participate in the process? ☐ ☐

This can be accomplished by _____

_____ .

4. Do you equally consider and evaluate ALL marketing communications forms that might effectively reach and touch the consumer at each step along their path to becoming a customer? Do these include advertising, direct marketing, marketing and corporate public relations, promotions, event sponsorships, packaging, and personal selling? ☐ ☐

This can be accomplished by _____

_____ .

5. Is there either a single "quarterback" or a team that can effectively manage all of your marketing communications efforts and judge them equally based on their merits, rather than on "the way it's always been done in the past"? ☐ ☐

   This can be accomplished by _____

   _____ .

6. Does your IMC program have at least one B-I-G idea that will help you stand out from your competitors? ☐ ☐

   This can be accomplished by _____

   _____ .

7. Do you have a "Customer Contact Strategy" that considers ALL vehicles that will deliver your messages as well as the messages themselves? Does it focus on the nontraditional as well as on the traditional media vehicles? Does it zero in on the environment, the time, and the place where you can best contact the members of your target audience? ☐ ☐

   This can be accomplished by _____

   _____ .

8. Do you capitalize on the long-term value of your customers by building relationships with them? Do you develop a database of everyone who has contact with your company in some significant way? ☐ ☐

   This can be accomplished by _____

   _____ .

9. Do you systematically evaluate your marketing communications program in terms of its delivery of a measurable response? Do you build on its strengths and determine what needs to be improved upon? ☐ ☐

   This can be accomplished by _____

   _____ .

The Ben Franklin
Advertising Option Evaluator

Ben Franklin developed a very simple technique to evaluate the pros and cons of any set of circumstances:

First, he divided a sheet of paper in half.

Second, he listed all the factors supporting a given position on the pro side and all of the factors opposing it on the con side.

Third, he "weighed" each pro against each con. Whichever side outweighed the other determined his course of action.

The Ben Franklin Advertising Option Evaluator lets you apply this same technique in deciding whether or not to invest in a given advertising opportunity or try a new marketing communications approach.

ADVERTISING OPTION

Pros	Cons
1. _____	1. _____
2. _____	2. _____
3. _____	3. _____
4. _____	4. _____
5. _____	5. _____
6. _____	6. _____
7. _____	7. _____
8. _____	8. _____
9. _____	9. _____
10. _____	10. _____

The Advertising Effectiveness Idea Provoker

Before you begin to solve a problem or come up with a new idea, you must first define your problem. You must look at what you are doing now and determine how well it is accomplishing what you have set out for it to do. *The Advertising Effectiveness Idea Provoker* is a first step in this process. It is aimed at uncovering any concerns you might have about your advertising program. These concerns can then act as a springboard to help you develop a new idea. Rather than advertising, it might even direct you to one of the many other marketing communications avenues.

Read the following statements and fill in the blank space at the end.

☐ I am basically satisfied with my advertising program.

☐ It appears to showcase my product (or service) well.

☐ It seems to be conveying to my customers what I want to tell them.

☐ It seems to be efficient.

☐ I believe it is doing an effective job.

☐ I only wish that _____

_____

_____

_____

_____

7

Coming Up with a New Idea: Part I

A successful business must constantly develop new ideas to communicate to the consumer. With appreciation to James Webb Young, here is a technique that has proven helpful to many who struggle daily to come up with that big, new, creative idea for media, research, or promotion.

First...... Gather together absolutely everything that can possibly help you. Search your own mind, dig through all of your files, and seek whatever might be available from other outside sources.

Second.... Examine all of this information and think about how each piece relates to every other piece *and* to your problem. Massage the material well and look at it from every angle.

Third..... "Out of sight, out of mind." Forget about your problem and go do something else. While your conscious mind is engaged in some other activity, your subconscious will have a chance to work for you in peace and quiet. Don't rush the process...be patient and relax.

Fourth.... "That's it!"...you will suddenly shout as the new concept comes to you often in the most unexpected place at the most unexpected time.

Fifth...... Now the work of refining your idea begins. When the joy of discovery has died down, begin to work with your newly conceived concept. Build upon it, refine it, try it out, until it becomes that new workable, winning idea.

Coming Up with a New Idea: Part II

While there is no single magic formula for coming up with a new idea, it helps to have a workable structure within which to plan. The structure should lead you smoothly along the path to a solution. This questioning approach has proven its worth many times.

1. What do your prospects want?

   _____

   _____

2. What do they want to know about?

   _____

   _____

3. Where do they turn for help?

   _____

   _____

4. What turns them off?

   _____

   _____

5. What turns them on?

   _____

   _____

6. How can you be involved in turning them on?

   _____

   _____

Coming Up with a New Idea: Part III

Sometimes you try and try and just can't come up with that new idea. Your mind needs a few gentle nudges. When you find yourself in this predicament, try these idea starters.

1. Can you break a rule and do the unexpected?

   How?_____

   _____

2. Can you make someone say "Why didn't I think of that?"

   How?_____

   _____

3. Can you combine two small ideas into one big one?

   How?_____

   _____

4. Can you associate the unknown with the known?

   How?_____

   _____

5. Can you associate the untried with the accepted?

   How?_____

   _____

6. Can you associate the traditional with the new?

   How?_____

   _____

Coming Up with a New Idea: Part III

7. Can you demonstrate something?

    How?_____

    _____

8. Can you appeal to the sense of sight?

    How?_____

    _____

9. Can you appeal to the sense of sound?

    How?_____

    _____

10. Can you appeal to the sense of smell?

    How?_____

    _____

11. Can you modify *when* something is normally done?

    How?_____

    _____

12. Can you modify *how* something is normally done?

    How?_____

    _____

13. Anything else?

    How?_____

    _____

Developing New Ideas in a Group: 11 Reminders

Have you ever wrestled with a problem all by yourself, only to have someone say "Why don't we . . . ?" Chances are you had your answer. The best ideas often come about when minds meet in an idea-generating session. But a productive session must encourage, not hinder, the thought process. These 11 reminders will help you reach the best ideas every time.

1. Make certain that your meeting place is comfortable and informal.

2. When you are trying to nourish the mind, you must not neglect the body. Have plenty of beverages and snacks around.

3. Select a good leader who will act as your "tour director."

4. Clearly define the problem when the meeting begins.

5. Set an agenda and time schedule and stick to it.

6. Keep detailed notes of all the ideas that are expressed.

7. Permit no criticism of any ideas or negative reactions to suggestions.

8. Let one idea build on and expand into another.

9. Keep all the participants actively involved in making contributions.

10. Encourage an off-the-wall, free-wheeling discussion. You are concerned here with the quantity, not the quality, of ideas.

11. After the meeting is over, apply your normal business judgment in sifting through all of the ideas. Target the best prospects and develop them.

11

Marketing a New Product? A 15-Point Early Warning System

Each year, companies introduce thousands of new products or services. Unfortunately, only a small percentage of them will succeed. Often, no real consumer need or desire exists for them. In other cases, a market may exist, but a business cannot be developed. This *15-Point Early Warning System* will help you evaluate whether or not to consider developing a new product or service.

	YES	NO
1. Is there a need or a consumer desire for the product?	☐	☐
2. Is it practical?	☐	☐
3. Is it unique?	☐	☐
4. Is the price right?	☐	☐
5. Is it a good value for the money?	☐	☐
6. Can your company make money on the product?	☐	☐
7. Does it appeal to a wide enough market?	☐	☐
8. Or, is there a smaller market segment that is anxious to have it?	☐	☐
9. Does it have a long potential life, or is it just a fad?	☐	☐
10. If it is a fad, can it make a short-term profit?	☐	☐
11. How great is the threat of competition?	☐	☐
12. Is there a ready, reputable, and reliable facility to manufacture, package, and get it to market?	☐	☐
13. Does it have a market that can be effectively and efficiently reached by one or more marketing communications forms?	☐	☐
14. Is it legal?	☐	☐
15. Is the payoff worth the time and money involved?	☐	☐

Part II

Creating the Messages

Effective advertising wins sales and an increased share of your customers' pocketbooks. If it also wins creative awards, so much the better—but a shelf of awards should not be your primary goal. Advertising that sells begins with a carefully spelled-out road map called the Communications Strategy Statement. It considers the customers you want to reach...the benefits your product or service will deliver to them...and the impact you want your advertising to have on them. The 17 checklists and charts in Part II will guide you in developing the Communications Strategy Statement and then executing a selling print or electronic media message.

12. The Communications Strategy Statement Planning Worksheet

13. Consumer Benefit Evaluator

14. 31 Ways in Which Advertising Appeals to the Consumer

15. 35 Ways in Which Advertising Gets Attention & Communicates

16. A Road Map for Moving from an Idea to a Message That Sells

17. Good Ads & Bad Ads: 9 Characteristics

18. 9 Tips for Creating More Effective Print Ads

19. How to Avoid the Most Common Mistakes in Writing Copy

20. 10 Keys to Effective Yellow Pages Advertising

21. 12 Guidelines to Effective Outdoor Signage

22. 6 Simple Tips for In-Store Customer Contacts

23. Guidelines for Creating TV Commercials That Sell

24. A Last-Minute Checkup on Your TV Storyboard

25. The 14 Key Values of Infomercials

26. Guidelines for Creating Radio Commercials That Sell

27. The Local Advertising Idea-Starter Kit

28. Should You Sponsor a Video?

12 The Communications Strategy Statement Planning Worksheet

Before you write word one of advertising copy, you must review all of the research and analyze all of the facts on your product or service and its market, customers, and competition. From this background, you will put together a single-page Communications Strategy Statement. It clearly and concisely identifies the purpose of your advertising, who you want to reach, what you want to convey to your audience, and how you want your message to be received. *The Communications Strategy Statement Planning Worksheet* provides you with a format and instructions for preparing this important document. Significantly, it can be applied to all marketing communications forms, not only advertising.

Purpose:

A brief statement of what you want the advertising to accomplish or what you want the consumer to do after exposure to the message.

_____

_____

_____

_____

Target Consumer:

A series of short descriptive phrases that define to whom you want to talk in demographic, psychographic, lifestyle, and/or purchase behavior terms.

_____

_____

_____

_____

Key Benefits:

A clear and simple statement of those real or perceived consumer needs and wants the product or service will satisfy or the consumer's problem that the product or service will solve better than will its competition.

_____

_____

_____

_____

The Communications Strategy Statement Planning Worksheet

Reason Why: Those significant and unique qualities that will convince the target consumer that the product or service can and will deliver the promised benefits.

_____

_____

_____

_____

Tone: The feeling, style, or approach of the advertising that will create a living personality for the product or service.

_____

_____

_____

_____

The Consumer "Take Away":   The total reaction you want from the consumer—in the consumer's own words—after seeing or hearing the message. Did you get through?

_____

_____

_____

_____

Consumer Benefit Evaluator

Every marketing communications effort must focus on those benefits that the product or service will deliver to the consumer. An important step in the process is for the marketer to examine the features of the product or service and determine their importance to the consumer. These features should then be compared to those of the competition. Finally, the marketer must determine where the product or service holds a competitive advantage over the competition. The *Consumer Benefit Evaluator* will help move this process along.

My Important Features	Similar Features By Competition		My Competitive Advantage
	YES	NO	
_____	☐	☐	_____
_____	☐	☐	_____
_____	☐	☐	_____
_____	☐	☐	_____
_____	☐	☐	_____
_____	☐	☐	_____
_____	☐	☐	_____
_____	☐	☐	_____
_____	☐	☐	_____
_____	☐	☐	_____
_____	☐	☐	_____
_____	☐	☐	_____
_____	☐	☐	_____
_____	☐	☐	_____
_____	☐	☐	_____

31 Ways in Which Advertising Appeals to the Consumer

To successfully communicate with the consumer, advertising must appeal to the individual's needs, wants, desires, hopes, and ambitions. In developing advertising strategies, use this checklist to note appeals used by you and your competition, and then check off appeals you might consider using in the future.

	Appeals Used by Competitors	Appeals We Use	Appeals We Might Use
1. Taste or hunger	☐	☐	☐
2. Comfort	☐	☐	☐
3. Beauty	☐	☐	☐
4. Attractiveness to others	☐	☐	☐
5. Well-being of loved ones	☐	☐	☐
6. Adventure or bravery	☐	☐	☐
7. Social status	☐	☐	☐
8. Approval of others	☐	☐	☐
9. Superiority over others	☐	☐	☐
10. Physical well-being	☐	☐	☐
11. Security	☐	☐	☐
12. Fear	☐	☐	☐
13. Fun and games	☐	☐	☐
14. Economy	☐	☐	☐

31 Ways in Which Advertising Appeals to the Consumer

	Appeals Used by Competitors	Appeals We Use	Appeals We Might Use
15. Efficiency	☐	☐	☐
16. Cleanliness	☐	☐	☐
17. Safety	☐	☐	☐
18. Happiness	☐	☐	☐
19. Romance and/or sex	☐	☐	☐
20. Excitement	☐	☐	☐
21. Rest	☐	☐	☐
22. Ambition	☐	☐	☐
23. Sympathy	☐	☐	☐
24. Guilt	☐	☐	☐
25. Avoidance of pain	☐	☐	☐
26. Entertainment	☐	☐	☐
27. Curiosity	☐	☐	☐
28. Hope	☐	☐	☐
29. Dependability	☐	☐	☐
30. Durability	☐	☐	☐
31. Peace	☐	☐	☐

35 Ways in Which Advertising Gets Attention & Communicates

Advertising uses many different techniques and combinations of techniques to attract attention and communicate with the consumer. This checklist focuses on the variety of devices available to both you and your competitors, and helps you to consider new options for future campaigns.

	Techniques Used by Competitors	Techniques We Use	Techniques We Might Use
1. Humor	☐	☐	☐
2. Real-life dramatizations	☐	☐	☐
3. Slices of life	☐	☐	☐
4. Testimonials	☐	☐	☐
5. Guarantees	☐	☐	☐
6. Comparisons	☐	☐	☐
7. Problem solving	☐	☐	☐
8. Characters	☐	☐	☐
9. Talking heads	☐	☐	☐
10. Recommendations	☐	☐	☐
11. Reasons why	☐	☐	☐
12. Facts	☐	☐	☐
13. News	☐	☐	☐
14. Emotion	☐	☐	☐
15. Cartoons	☐	☐	☐
16. Animation	☐	☐	☐
17. Charts	☐	☐	☐

35 Ways in Which Advertising Gets Attention & Communicates

	Techniques Used by Competitors	Techniques We Use	Techniques We Might Use
18. Computer graphics	☐	☐	☐
19. Claymation	☐	☐	☐
20. Music	☐	☐	☐
21. Symbols	☐	☐	☐
22. Animals	☐	☐	☐
23. Contests and sweepstakes	☐	☐	☐
24. Offers	☐	☐	☐
25. Exaggeration	☐	☐	☐
26. Glamour	☐	☐	☐
27. Personalities	☐	☐	☐
28. Spokespersons	☐	☐	☐
29. 800 and 900 numbers	☐	☐	☐
30. The product alone	☐	☐	☐
31. The product in use	☐	☐	☐
32. Different uses for the product	☐	☐	☐
33. Effects of *not* using the product	☐	☐	☐
34. Before and after	☐	☐	☐
35. The package as the star	☐	☐	☐

16 A Road Map for Moving from an Idea to a Message That Sells

Once you are convinced you have that great advertising idea, your work is just beginning. You must translate the idea into an advertisement or commercial that sells. *A Road Map for Moving from an Idea to a Message That Sells* is a "moving checklist." Refer to it frequently, as you would to a road map. Next to each point, check whether you are keeping on the right road. Then, in the space beneath each point, indicate where you seem to be taking a detour and what you need to do to get back on track.

	YES	NO
1. Have you learned everything you could possibly learn about your product or service?	☐	☐
2. Have you learned everything you could possibly learn about your customer—the person who will use, buy, or influence the purchase of your product or service?	☐	☐
3. Have you written to your customer as you would write to a real-life person, and not just a research statistic?	☐	☐
4. Have you promised to deliver a real benefit to your customer and then backed this up with real reasons why he or she will receive this benefit?	☐	☐
5. Have you recognized that your customer's time is valuable by getting right to the point?	☐	☐

	YES	NO
6. Have you made certain that what you said relates specifically to you and not to your competition?	☐	☐
7. Have you avoided saying more than was necessary?	☐	☐
8. Have you written with excitement and enthusiasm so your customer will say . . . "They really believe in what they're selling"?	☐	☐
9. Have you rewarded your customer by making it easy and fun for him or her to spend time with your advertising?	☐	☐
10. Have you never forgotten for a moment that the product or service is the star of your advertising, not the advertising itself?	☐	☐

Good Ads & Bad Ads: 9 Characteristics

What is a good ad?

What is a bad ad?

Everyone may have a different definition of good and bad. However, to be successful, an ad must grab consumers and hold on to them. It must touch the consumers' emotions. It must convince consumers that what it is offering is something they absolutely, positively cannot do without.

There is "magic" that goes into a good ad. Even more magic goes into a great ad.

When you look at advertising, consider these nine key ways in which a good ad may be distinguished from a bad ad. If any of the nine bad characteristics apply to your ad, chances are it is a bad ad. And remember. Don't just be satisfied with good. Strive for great!

Good Ad	Bad Ad
Dynamic	Undynamic
Sensitive	Arrogant
Tasteful	Tasteless
Vibrant	Lifeless
Exciting	Boring
Relevant	Irrelevant
Grabbing	Unnoticeable
Enhancing	Poison
Treasurable	Trashable

9 Tips for Creating More Effective Print Ads

An effective magazine or newspaper ad wins awards from the consumer's pocketbook—not just from art competitions. While there is no simple formula for creating advertising that automatically sells, the following tips are fundamental to the success of any ad. If you cannot answer "Yes" to every one of these questions, the odds say you will have considerable trouble communicating your message from the magazine or newspaper page to the consumer's active mind. To prevent this, take a moment to think about how you can change each "No" to a "Yes."

	YES	NO
1. Is the message clear at a glance? Can you quickly tell what the ad is all about?	☐	☐
2. Is there a benefit in the headline?	☐	☐
3. Does the illustration support the headline?	☐	☐
4. Does the first line of copy support or explain the copy or illustration?	☐	☐
5. Is the ad easy to read and easy to follow?	☐	☐

9 Tips for Creating More Effective Print Ads

	YES	NO
6. Is the type large and legible?	☐	☐

_____

_____

7. Is the advertiser clearly identified?	☐	☐

_____

_____

8. Have all excess words, phrases, or even ideas been deleted?	☐	☐

_____

_____

9. If there is a coupon or clip-out, is it easy to remove or get?	☐	☐

_____

_____

Source: *Strategic Advertising Campaigns*, by Don E. Schultz and Beth E. Barnes (1995).

How to Avoid the Most Common Mistakes in Writing Copy

In their book *Which Ad Pulled Best?*, Philip Ward Burton and Scott C. Purvis isolated six factors that tended to separate copy that generated strong consumer response from copy that was less effective. Use this 6-point checklist to monitor your own advertising. Note those areas where you feel your copy is falling short and comment on how it might be improved.

	YES	NO
1. Does the copy offer a big benefit?	☐	☐
Suggested Improvement: _____		
_____		
2. Is the copy easy to see and read?	☐	☐
Suggested Improvement: _____		
_____		
3. Have you established audience identity so it is easy for the readers to see themselves in and involved by the advertising?	☐	☐
Suggested Improvement: _____		
_____		
4. Does the copy attract the audience by being new?	☐	☐
Suggested Improvement: _____		
_____		
5. Is the copy believable?	☐	☐
Suggested Improvement: _____		
_____		
6. Has the copy stressed what is unique?	☐	☐
Suggested Improvement: _____		
_____		

Source: *Which Ad Pulled Best?* by Philip Ward Burton and Scott C. Purvis (1993).

10 Keys to Effective Yellow Pages Advertising

The Yellow Pages is the lifeline that ties a company to its customers and potential customers. As the nation's fourth largest advertising medium, it is the place consumers go to when they want to buy and want to know where to buy. To effectively communicate, a Yellow Pages ad should adhere to these ten guidelines. How well does your ad meet the criteria? How can you make certain that it does?

	YES	NO

1. The headline should focus on what the business offers and not just on its name. ☐ ☐

   This can be accomplished by _____

   _____

2. The typeface should be simple and bold. ☐ ☐

   This can be accomplished by _____

   _____

3. The ad must not be complicated and wordy. ☐ ☐

   This can be accomplished by _____

   _____

4. The visuals should be striking and "grabbing." ☐ ☐

   This can be accomplished by _____

   _____

5. The ad must be placed in the right heading or headings where consumers might go for the product or service. ☐ ☐

   This can be accomplished by _____

   _____

10 Keys to Effective Yellow Pages Advertising

6. The ad should reflect positively on both the image and personality of the business. ☐ ☐

   This can be accomplished by _____

   _____

7. The ad should include those special features of the business that might attract the consumer. ☐ ☐

   This can be accomplished by _____

   _____

8. The location and phone number should be large and clear. ☐ ☐

   This can be accomplished by _____

   _____

9. For retail businesses in hard-to-find locations, the ad should show how to get there. ☐ ☐

   This can be accomplished by _____

   _____

10. Because the directory is published only once a year, an ad should feature Audiotex (where available) to build in timeliness. ☐ ☐

    This can be accomplished by _____

    _____

12 Guidelines to Effective Outdoor Signage

The consumer on the move, whether traveling on foot, in a car, or via public transportation, is exposed to many outdoor media forms. To effectively communicate with this consumer, outdoor signage should adhere to these 12 key guidelines. How well does your signage meet these criteria? If it doesn't, how can you make certain that it does?

	YES	NO
1. It is easy to see and read at a high speed.	☐	☐

This can be accomplished by _____

_____

| 2. The typeface is simple and bold. | ☐ | ☐ |

This can be accomplished by _____

_____

| 3. It does not require the viewer to squint or strain. | ☐ | ☐ |

This can be accomplished by _____

_____

| 4. The visuals are striking and "grabbing." | ☐ | ☐ |

This can be accomplished by _____

_____

| 5. The background colors do not blur into the words and pictures. | ☐ | ☐ |

This can be accomplished by _____

_____

| 6. All of the visual elements reinforce one another and are instantly memorable. | ☐ | ☐ |

This can be accomplished by _____

_____

12 Guidelines to Effective Outdoor Signage

	YES	NO
	☐	☐

7. The product, package, and related icons are easy to recognize.

   This can be accomplished by _____

   _____

8. Where appropriate, it makes use of a unique size or shape.

   This can be accomplished by _____

   _____

9. It triggers an action response (Exit on 123), it provokes a laugh, it answers a question, or it "burns in" an easily remembered number to call (1-800 CALL RON).

   This can be accomplished by _____

   _____

10. The total effect is a board or sign that stands out from its surroundings.

   This can be accomplished by _____

   _____

11. It takes advantage of opportunities to reinforce a message the consumer may have received via another medium.

   This can be accomplished by _____

   _____

12. Using seven words or less, it very succinctly conveys at a glance everything it needs to say.

   This can be accomplished by _____

   _____

6 Simple Tips for In-Store Customer Contacts

More than two-thirds of all purchase decisions are made only after the customer has entered the store. It is therefore not surprising that marketers continue to increase and enhance their use of in-store media. Whether your message is a simple sign on a shopping cart or an elaborate end-aisle display, consider how each of these six tips can enhance your contacts with the consumer.

	YES	NO

1. It is easy to see and read by the customer on the go. ☐ ☐

   This can be enhanced by _____

   _____

2. It is simple to understand. ☐ ☐

   This can be enhanced by _____

   _____

3. It is memorable. ☐ ☐

   This can be enhanced by _____

   _____

4. Its message quickly relays a "competitive edge" benefit for the consumer in terms of price, quality, a special offer, etc. ☐ ☐

   This can be enhanced by _____

   _____

5. It seeks a unique visual (or audio) approach to communicate with the consumer. ☐ ☐

   This can be enhanced by _____

   _____

6. It stands out from all other signs and displays for other products. ☐ ☐

   This can be enhanced by _____

   _____

23 Guidelines for Creating TV Commercials That Sell

Every day, the average American spends more hours with television than with any other medium. At the same time, advertisers are faced with rapidly escalating television costs and consumers who can "Zap" out and "Zip" through their commercials. *Guidelines for Creating TV Commercials That Sell* will help you develop commercials that will rack up sales—not just creative awards.

	YES	NO
1. Have you done your basic research first and gathered all the facts on your product or service *and* the competition? Suggested Improvement: _____ _____	☐	☐
2. Have you emphasized your main selling point—your single, strongest, most provocative idea? Suggested Improvement: _____ _____	☐	☐
3. Have you made your commercial relevant to your viewers' wants and needs and respected their sensitivities and intelligence? Suggested Improvement: _____ _____	☐	☐
4. Have you "interrupted" the consumer and gotten his or her attention fast—and kept it? Suggested Improvement: _____ _____	☐	☐
5. Have you let the viewer know "What's in it for me?" Suggested Improvement: _____ _____	☐	☐

Guidelines for Creating TV Commercials That Sell

	YES	NO

6. Have you matched the format, structure, and style of your commercial so they are all compatible with each other and with your product or service? ☐ ☐

   Suggested Improvement: _____

   _____

7. Have you matched the video with the audio so as not to confuse the viewer? ☐ ☐

   Suggested Improvement: _____

   _____

8. Are you on track with your strategy statement and marketing objectives? Do you clearly demonstrate the benefits of the product or service? ☐ ☐

   Suggested Improvement: _____

   _____

9. Because television is primarily a visual medium, have you avoided wasting words? ☐ ☐

   Suggested Improvement: _____

   _____

10. Have you kept your commercial simple and avoided cramming your spot with too many scenes, too much action, or too many effects? ☐ ☐

    Suggested Improvement: _____

    _____

11. Have you written clearly and conversationally? ☐ ☐

    Suggested Improvement: _____

    _____

12. Have you clearly identified your product or service and implanted the brand name strongly in the viewer's mind? ☐ ☐

    Suggested Improvement: _____

    _____

Guidelines for Creating TV Commercials That Sell

	YES	NO

13. Have you timed your commercial to make sure it is not so fast that it loses its dramatic appeal and leaves the viewer behind? ☐ ☐

Suggested Improvement: _____

_____

14. Have you treated news as news if your product is new or has a new feature? ☐ ☐

Suggested Improvement: _____

_____

15. Have you repeated yourself to help register your selling idea? ☐ ☐

Suggested Improvement: _____

_____

16. Have you concentrated on writing and not on drawing? ☐ ☐

Suggested Improvement: _____

_____

17. Are you prepared to revise, revise, revise? ☐ ☐

Suggested Improvement: _____

_____

18. Have (or will) you give some free rein to the producer to make the commercial even better? ☐ ☐

Suggested Improvement: _____

_____

Source: *The Radio & Television Commercial*, by Albert C. Book, Norman D. Cary, and Stanley I. Tannenbaum (1984).

24

A Last-Minute Checkup on Your TV Storyboard

Speak now or forever hold your peace! That's how every commercial producer feels before shooting starts. And just as an automobile needs a careful inspection prior to a long trip, the TV storyboard needs a final checkup before production begins. A thorough checkup will save you time and money—and can mean the difference between great success and dismal failure in the final product.

	YES	NO

1. Is there a single central message or idea? ☐ ☐

   Action to Take: _____

   _____

2. Is the message you want to communicate clearly and explicitly stated? ☐ ☐

   Action to Take: _____

   _____

3. Can you communicate the actions you want in the desired atmosphere within the time available? ☐ ☐

   Action to Take: _____

   _____

4. Does the opening shot set the stage and convey only what is essential to the understanding of what follows? ☐ ☐

   Action to Take: _____

   _____

5. Do the opening seconds involve and attract the viewer in a way that is relevant to the viewer and the product? ☐ ☐

   Action to Take: _____

   _____

A Last-Minute Checkup on Your TV Storyboard

6. Do the shots progress in a "logical" order (or "illogically logical" order), and does each successive shot advance the story and add to the viewer's knowledge of what is going on?   ☐   ☐

Action to Take: _____

_____

7. Are the pictures explicit, simple, and single-minded?   ☐   ☐

Action to Take: _____

_____

8. Do the words reinforce the pictures or are they merely redundant?   ☐   ☐

Action to Take: _____

_____

9. Are "supers" in sync with the audio so that they say the same thing at the same time?   ☐   ☐

Action to Take: _____

_____

10. Are the words clear and meaningful *in themselves* and will they be understood by a majority of the viewers?   ☐   ☐

Action to Take: _____

_____

11. Are the words clear and meaningful at each point in the story, or do they depend for their meaning or impact on something that has not yet occurred in the story?   ☐   ☐

Action to Take: _____

_____

A Last-Minute Checkup on Your TV Storyboard

	YES	NO

12. Is the copy structured to maximize the impact of the visuals? ☐ ☐

   Action to Take: _____

   _____

13. Could the viewer repeat the story of the commercial without mentioning the product (so it seems as if the product came out of left field and the story is an irrelevant attention getter)? ☐ ☐

   Action to Take: _____

   _____

14. Does the product enter at the *right moment* and not just at the first moment? ☐ ☐

   Action to Take: _____

   _____

15. If it is a :60, could you cut it to a :30 (or if a :30, could it be cut to a :15)? The point is...how much does the extra time really add to the idea? ☐ ☐

   Action to Take: _____

   _____

16. Is the commercial story believable? If no, is the selling message believable within the unbelievable or exaggerated story? ☐ ☐

   Action to Take: _____

   _____

Source: *Creating Effective TV Commercials*, by Huntley Baldwin (1982).

25

The 14 Key Values
of Infomercials

In the early days of television, the 60-second commercial was the norm. But TV costs increased, and marketers sought to expose their messages to more different people. As a result, 60 seconds gave way to 30 seconds and finally the 15-second message came into being. Today, however, a new commercial form has moved in the exact opposite direction. The "infomercial," often 30 minutes in length, provides marketers with the opportunity to stand out from the crowd, deliver an in-depth, personal sales message, and even sell a product directly to the consumer. These *14 Key Values of Infomercials* will help you determine whether this marketing communications form is right for you. Interact with this checklist and indicate how important each value is to you.

1. An infomercial offers a television environment in which to deliver an extended, personal sales message.

   This infomercial value is important to me because _____

   _____

2. An infomercial can communicate a very long and complex subject.

   This infomercial value is important to me because _____

   _____

3. An infomercial allows you to deliver your message in a relaxed, even homey, setting.

   This infomercial value is important to me because _____

   _____

4. An infomercial is a marketing communication vehicle that the consumer actually chooses to watch.

   This infomercial value is important to me because _____

   _____

5. An infomercial can be taped by the consumer for playback at another time.

   This infomercial value is important to me because _____

   _____

The 14 Key Values of Infomercials

6. An infomercial can generate revenue through direct sales.

   This infomercial value is important to me because _____

   _____

7. An infomercial can provide you with a communication edge over your competition.

   This infomercial value is important to me because _____

   _____

8. An informercial is a vehicle for which you can determine a measurable response.

   This infomercial value is important to me because _____

   _____

9. An infomercial can differentiate one brand from another.

   This infomercial value is important to me because _____

   _____

10. An infomercial can showcase and offer in-depth news about a product or service.

    This infomercial value is important to me because _____

    _____

11. An infomercial can educate the consumer about the benefits of a product or service.

    This infomercial value is important to me because _____

    _____

12. An infomercial can serve as the focal point for a promotional event.

    This infomercial value is important to me because _____

    _____

13. An infomercial can act as a "sales warm-up" and encourage viewers to call for further information or to set up a sales visit.

    This infomercial value is important to me because _____

    _____

14. An infomercial can urge prospects to buy a product at a local store.

    This infomercial value is important to me because _____

    _____

26 Guidelines for Creating Radio Commercials That Sell

Radio is everywhere. It is in the home, in the car, on the beach. It rests on the teen's shoulder, and it is stuck in the jogger's ear. Today, radio is even piped into the supermarket providing the closest-to-purchase exposure of any advertising medium. Refer to *Guidelines for Creating Radio Commercials That Sell* before you start writing, refer to it as you write, and then use it for one final checkup before you go into production.

	YES	NO

1. Have you written conversationally for the ear so that the commercial is *visually* and *conceptually* clear through words and sounds? ☐ ☐

   Suggested Improvements: _____

   _____

2. Have you involved the listener and captured and excited his or her imagination? ☐ ☐

   Suggested Improvements: _____

   _____

3. Did you stick to one, strong, central idea? ☐ ☐

   Suggested Improvements: _____

   _____

4. Have you singled out your prospect and written just to him or her? ☐ ☐

   Suggested Improvements: _____

   _____

5. Does the commercial sound the way your prospect speaks? ☐ ☐

   Suggested Improvements: _____

   _____

	YES	NO

6. Did you set the mood for your product based upon *how* you want the listener to hear and react? ☐ ☐

Suggested Improvements: _____

_____

7. Have you remembered your mnemonics—those words, music, and effects that can register in your prospect's mind? ☐ ☐

Suggested Improvements: _____

_____

8. Have you gotten attention fast? ☐ ☐

Suggested Improvements: _____

_____

9. Is the brand clearly identified, and will the product's name be quickly and easily registered in the consumer's mind? ☐ ☐

Suggested Improvements: _____

_____

10. Have you avoided overwriting and crowding your spot with too much copy? ☐ ☐

Suggested Improvements: _____

_____

11. Have you made your appeal clear? ☐ ☐

Suggested Improvements: _____

_____

Creating Radio Commercials That Sell

	YES	NO
12. If your message is news, have you made it sound important?	☐	☐

Suggested Improvements: _____

_____

13. Have you kept a friendly feeling throughout your message? ☐ ☐

Suggested Improvements: _____

_____

14. If your spot is supposed to be humorous, is it really funny? ☐ ☐

Suggested Improvements: _____

_____

15. Have you considered multiplying your television impressions by using your TV audio in your radio spot? ☐ ☐

Suggested Improvements: _____

_____

16. Have you given your listener something to do—to react to your message, to remember it, to act upon it? ☐ ☐

Suggested Improvements: _____

_____

17. Once is not enough, so have you repeated anything the listener might not get the first (or second) time? ☐ ☐

Suggested Improvements: _____

_____

Source: *The Radio & Television Commercial*, by Albert C. Book, Norman D. Cary, and Stanley I. Tannenbaum (1984).

27

The Local Advertising
Idea-Starter Kit

With limited financial resources, the local advertiser must continually rely on his or her own imagination for the creation of effective selling concepts. Sometimes, the most difficult task is coming up with that first idea. *The Local Advertising Idea-Starter Kit* includes 104 ideas covering 42 product and service categories. The challenge is the "blank space" in which you should add your own creativity. As you do so, focus on those ideas that will most effectively touch your customers in the highly competitive communications environment of the 1990s and beyond.

Air Conditioning and Heating Companies

Home Insulation and Energy Conservation _____

_____

_____

_____

Airlines

Exercises for the Business Traveler _____

Great Restaurants around the Country (World) _____

Getting Ready for Your Vacation _____

_____

_____

_____

Appliance Stores

Household Safety Tips _____

Energy-Saving Tips _____

_____

_____

_____

Art Galleries and Dealers

What to Look for in Buying Art _____

_____

_____

_____

The Local Advertising Idea-Starter Kit

Automobile Dealers

Where to Go and How to Get There _____

How to Shop for a Car _____

_____

_____

_____

Automobile Supply Stores

Do-It-Yourself Video Car Manual _____

_____

_____

_____

Bakeries

Entertaining for the Holidays _____

Tips on Party Planning _____

_____

_____

_____

Banks and Savings and Loans

Personal Finance _____

The ABCs of Getting a Loan _____

The ABCs of the IRA _____

_____

_____

_____

Bedding Companies

Interpreting Your Dreams _____

_____

_____

_____

Boats and Marine Equipment

Boating Conditions in Your Area _____

Tips on Sailing _____

_____

_____

_____

Book Stores

Book Review of the Week _____

The Top 10 Books of the Week _____

_____

_____

_____

Building Material

How to Build Almost Anything _____

What to Keep in Your Garage _____

_____

_____

_____

Burglar Alarms and Security Systems

Safeguarding Your Valuables _____

Protecting Your Home against Intruders _____

_____

_____

_____

The Local Advertising Idea-Starter Kit

Clothing Stores

Community Fashion Shows _____

The Latest Fashions _____

Clothes for the Working Woman _____

How to Coordinate and Care for Your Wardrobe _____

_____

_____

_____

Cosmetics and Beauty Aids

Makeup and Beauty Hints _____

Taking Care of Your Face, Feet, and Hands _____

_____

_____

_____

Dental and Medical Services

Exercises at Your Desk _____

Foods for a Healthier You _____

Understanding the New Health Care Legislation _____

Kick the Smoking Habit _____

_____

_____

_____

Drugstores

Organizing Your Medicine Cabinet _____

Lists to Leave for the Babysitter _____

_____

_____

_____

The Local Advertising Idea-Starter Kit

Educational Institutions

Going Back to School after 30! _____

_____

_____

_____

Employment and Recruitment Agencies

How to Interview for a Job _____

Assessing Your Strengths and Weaknesses _____

Writing an Effective Resume _____

_____

_____

_____

Financial Services

Tips on Keeping Tax Records _____

Understanding the New Tax Laws _____

Tax Deductions You May Have Overlooked _____

The Stock Market Report _____

Planning the Family Budget _____

_____

_____

_____

Furniture Stores

Caring for Your Furniture _____

Arranging Furniture in Your Home _____

Interior Decorating on a Budget _____

_____

_____

_____

The Local Advertising Idea-Starter Kit

**Garden and
Lawn Supplies**

Planning Your Summer Garden _____

Caring for Your Garden _____

Loving Your Plants _____

New and Different Salads _____

_____

_____

_____

Grocery Stores

Holiday Food Ideas _____

Meals on a Budget _____

Recipes for the Working Woman _____

How to Fix a Last-Minute Dinner _____

Planning Your Shopping List _____

Summer Picnic Meals _____

Seasonal Food Specialties _____

_____

_____

_____

**Hardware
Dealers**

Complete Do-It-Yourself Manual _____

How to Repair Almost Anything _____

Organizing Your Kitchen _____

Women in the Hardware Store _____

_____

_____

_____

The Local Advertising Idea-Starter Kit

Health Food Stores

Eating for a Healthier Life _____

Putting Nutrition in Your Diet _____

_____

_____

_____

Hobby Shops

Things to Do on a Rainy Day _____

Fun for the Family _____

Hobbies in Your Town _____

_____

_____

Home Improvements and Remodeling

Remodeling on a Budget _____

Redoing the Kitchen and Bath _____

_____

_____

_____

Hotels and Motels

Spending the Weekend in Town _____

Entertainment Guide of the Week _____

_____

_____

_____

Insurance Agencies

How to Buy Insurance _____

How Much Insurance Is Enough _____

_____

_____

_____

The Local Advertising Idea-Starter Kit

Luggage Stores Packing the Most in the Least Space _____

Matching Your Luggage to Your Travel Needs _____

_____

_____

_____

Movers Getting Ready to Move _____

Last-Minute Moving Checklist _____

_____

_____

_____

Office Equipment Buying a Personal Computer _____

Organizing Your Workspace More Efficiently _____

_____

_____

_____

Pest Control and Exterminators The Warning Signs of Pest Danger _____

When to Call the Exterminator _____

_____

_____

_____

Photo Equipment Stores Photography Made Easy _____

How to Photograph Children _____

Choosing the Right Camera (Film) _____

_____

_____

The Local Advertising Idea-Starter Kit

Real Estate Firms

Video Home Tours _____

Round-the-Clock Cable Home Listings _____

_____

_____

_____

Restaurants

Favorite Meals of the Chef _____

Favorites of the Celebrities _____

_____

_____

_____

Service Stations

Getting Your Car Set for Winter (or Summer) _____

Safe Driving Tips _____

When Your Car Won't Start _____

_____

_____

_____

Sporting Goods Stores

High School Sports _____

Tips for (Golf, Tennis, etc.) _____

Sportswear Fashions _____

_____

_____

_____

The Local Advertising Idea-Starter Kit

Stereos and Hi-Fi's

Video Music Show (featuring local talent) _____

How to Shop for a Stereo _____

_____

_____

_____

Theaters

Entertainment Gossip News _____

Movie Trivia Quiz _____

_____

_____

_____

Travel Agencies

Vacations on a Budget _____

Where to Go for a Weekend _____

Exotic Spots to Visit _____

_____

_____

_____

Veterinarians

Taking Care of Your Dog or Cat _____

Taking Your Pet on Vacation _____

Training Your Dog or Cat _____

_____

_____

_____

28

Should You Sponsor a Video?

An increasing number of consumer and business-to-business marketers are actively communicating with their customers via video. This may involve development and/or sponsorship of programming related to their product, service, or corporate interests. Before investing money or time in such a venture, complete this checklist. Each question you answer "No" to represents a problem you will need to overcome if your video venture is to be a success.

Is There a Problem?

	YES	NO
1. Does the idea offer a potentially high level of consumer interest?	☐	☐

Why? _____

_____

2. Is the video product well conceived? Will it be well executed, and will it be compelling and exciting to view?	☐	☐

Why? _____

_____

3. Will the video communicate better than print in a highly visual manner?	☐	☐

Why? _____

_____

4. Is there a strong distribution facility that will move the video to its intended audience?	☐	☐

Why? _____

_____

5. Will the video be part of an extended total merchandising package that you offer?	☐	☐

Why? _____

_____

Part III

Maneuvering through the Media

Without a message delivery system, the finest ad is no more than a snapshot; the most outstanding commercial is only a home movie. The goal of media is to deliver your messages to your customers effectively and efficiently—and Part III's 20 checklists and charts will help you accomplish this. They focus on building and implementing a message delivery plan based upon practical, actionable objectives, and on determining which media will best meet these objectives. A step-by-step examination of what your plan is missing will help you develop creative new ways of using media. And you can evaluate how and whether any of the many new message delivery systems could impact on your business and on your customers.

29. Sound Media Management: 10 Principles

30. A Model for Media Planning

31. The Preplanning Process

32. Checking Up on Your Media Plan

33. Monitoring Your Agency's Media Capabilities

34. 105 Customer Contact Points from A to Z

35. The Media Value Checklist

36. 20 Points for Assessing the Value of Place-Based Media

37. Implementing a Media Buy

38. 35 Value-Added Media Opportunities

39. Guiding the Search for a Creative Media Concept

40. The Creative Media Pocket Planner

41. How to Evaluate TV Special Sponsorship Opportunities

42. Questions to Ask When Considering Sponsorship of an Event

43. How to Evaluate a New Media Opportunity

44. 11 Keys to the Success of a New Information Delivery System

45. Two-Way Interactivity: 11 Insights

46. Reaching Consumers in a High-Tech Environment: 12 Facts of Life

47. A Guide to 19 Key Media Terms

48. Customer Contact Reach Calculator

29

Sound Media Management: 10 Principles

Are you a sound media manager? This checklist gives you a chance to find out. Answer each question honestly. Then for each question to which you have answered "No," indicate what you might do to change your response to "Yes." Keep your completed self-analysis handy and refer to it often. In that way, you can monitor the degree to which you accomplish the goals of sound media management you have set for yourself.

	YES	NO
1. Are you a money manager who never forgets that the numbers in a media plan are backed by *real* dollars?	☐	☐
2. Are you careful to remember that effectiveness is primary and efficiency is not necessarily the key criterion?	☐	☐
3. Do you appreciate that all numbers are *estimates* based upon a sampling of the population and that they can swing up or down depending on the research technique, the time of year, and the particular sample chosen?	☐	☐
4. Are you creative? Do you think? Do you innovate?	☐	☐
5. Are you conversant with all media forms, and do you keep on top of the latest developments?	☐	☐

Sound Media Management: 10 Principles

	YES	NO
6. Do you evaluate all reasonable alternatives?	☐	☐

_____

_____

7. Do you constantly monitor the performance of your media plan's delivery, upgrade it when possible, and correct discrepancies immediately?	☐	☐

_____

_____

8. Do you keep all those with whom you work informed about the latest media trends?	☐	☐

_____

_____

9. Have you established and do you maintain a strong rapport with media suppliers?	☐	☐

_____

_____

10. Are you involved in the total marketing picture rather than just with those issues involving media matters? Do you seek to recommend marketing, creative, and/or new product ideas that can build your business?	☐	☐

_____

_____

Source: *Media Planning: A Practical Guide*, by Jim Surmanek (1985).

30

A Model for Media Planning

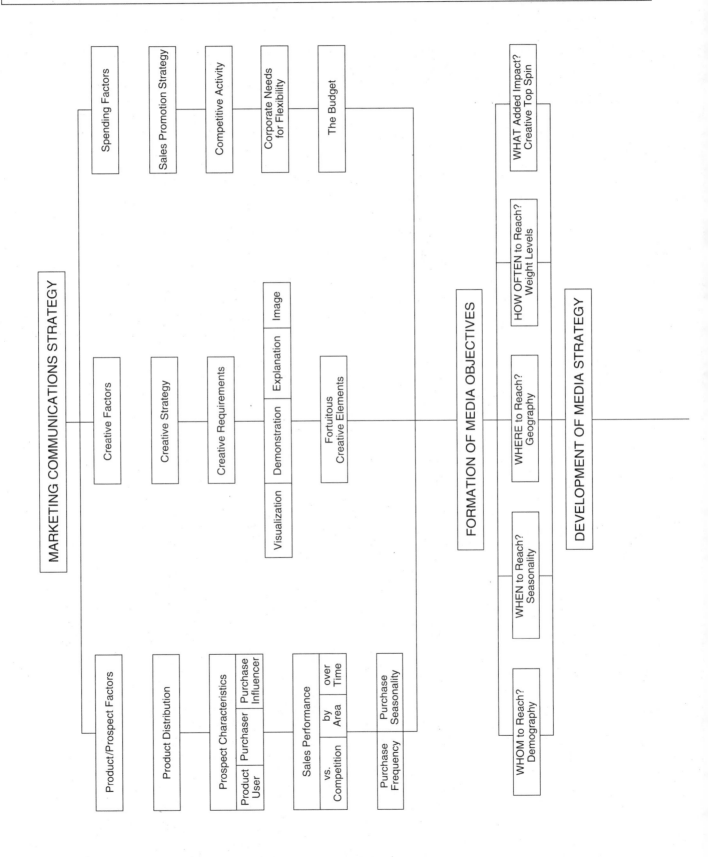

A Model for Media Planning

The media planning process begins with a thorough study of the marketing communications strategy. It continues by establishing a set of media objectives from which a media strategy is derived. From here, the full media plan is developed, after which the plan is implemented by buying and scheduling specific message delivery options.

A Model for Media Planning documents this process in a flow chart.

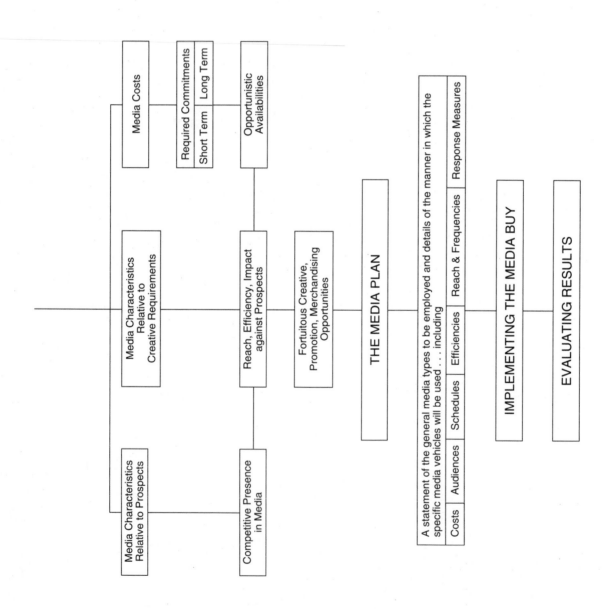

31

The Preplanning Process

The first step in any planning process is "preplanning." It gathers together those key client and agency representatives who should have input into the plan and who will later be asked to approve the plan or send it back to the drawing board. Everyone participating in the preplanning session must agree upon the key factors that will later impact on the building of the plan.

Preplanning is designed to improve planning and avoid confusion. It is an opportunity for everyone to "speak now or forever hold your peace!" Preplanning should be a part of every planning process, whether it involves creative, media, sales promotion, direct marketing, event marketing, etc. In this checklist, the focus is on media preplanning. At minimum, the preplanning session must reach agreement on the following issues:

	Agreement Is Reached?	
	YES	**NO**
1. Agreement as to what media is expected to accomplish as part of the marketing communications process.	☐	☐
2. Agreement as to who is the competition.	☐	☐
3. Agreement as to who is the prime target, including customers, purchase influencers, sales force, and others.	☐	☐
4. Agreement as to how the product will be positioned in the mind of the customer.	☐	☐
5. Agreement as to the communication/creative strategy that will be employed.	☐	☐
6. Agreement as to seasonal factors to be considered.	☐	☐
7. Agreement as to geographic factors to be considered.	☐	☐
8. Agreement as to what available research and marketing information should be considered.	☐	☐
9. Agreement as to what past media efforts have been successful and why.	☐	☐
10. Agreement as to what past media efforts have not been successful and why.	☐	☐

The Preplanning Process

	YES	NO
11. Agreement as to what creative elements should be considered.	☐	☐
12. Agreement as to what response mechanism(s) will (or should) be built into the plan.	☐	☐
13. Agreement as to how the plan will or should be tied to other elements of the marketing communications plan.	☐	☐
14. Agreement as to how the success of the plan will be evaluated.	☐	☐
15. Agreement as to any corporate policies that might affect the choice of media vehicles included in the plan.	☐	☐
16. Agreement as to anything else that might be overlooked but that should be included in the plan or in the presentation of the plan.	☐	☐

32

Checking Up on Your Media Plan

A media plan is put together with care and concern to accomplish certain objectives. The degree to which the plan succeeds depends upon whether these objectives are the correct ones, and, if so, whether the media plan successfully implements them. Use the following checklist to make certain that your media plan carries out the goals you have set for it.

	Is Our Objective on Target?	Does the Plan Implement It?
1. WHOM do we want to reach? Are we certain this is the correct target? Have we missed anyone who might be a significant product or service user, purchaser, or influencer?	☐	☐

Suggested Improvement: _____

_____

_____

2. WHEN do we want to reach them? Are we certain we are reaching them when they will not only be interested in our product or service but also be most interested in receiving our message? Have we considered not only what time of the year, but also what times of the week and what times of the day we should reach them?	☐	☐

Suggested Improvement: _____

_____

_____

3. WHERE do we want to reach them? Are we focusing on those geographic areas where our dollars can work most productively? Has the plan considered all of the regional and local marketing factors that influence the purchase and usage of our product or service? Have we considered how our market focus will impact upon key factors in the trade? Have we considered the value of reaching our target at home vs. at work vs. elsewhere?	☐	☐

Suggested Improvement: _____

_____

_____

4. HOW MANY do we need to reach? Are we reaching enough prospects with our message during a specific promotional period or within a specific time frame that relates to our product or service's purchase or usage cycle?	☐	☐

Suggested Improvement: _____

_____

_____

Checking Up on Your Media Plan

	Is Our Objective on Target?	Does the Plan Implement It?

5. HOW FREQUENTLY do we need to reach them? Are we reaching them often enough to make our point, yet not so often that we waste money that could more profitably be directed elsewhere? ☐ ☐

Suggested Improvement: _____

_____

_____

6. WHAT MEDIA provide the best environments and conditions under which to reach our prospects? Have we selected media that will enhance the delivery of our message? Will it help us stand out from the crowd and the clutter? ☐ ☐

Suggested Improvement: _____

_____

_____

7. AT WHAT COST do we reach our prospects? Are we spending too much to accomplish our objectives? Or are we spending so little that we are in essence "invisible"? Are we spending enough not only in total but also in each individual media vehicle so as to establish an effective presence? Have we considered not only the present activity of our competition, but also their anticipated future activity? ☐ ☐

Suggested Improvement: _____

_____

_____

8. IS ANYTHING MISSING...OR SHOULD ANYTHING BE DONE DIFFERENTLY? Have we looked at our media plan from all angles? Have we challenged it? Have we compared it with other reasonable alternatives? ☐ ☐

Suggested Improvement: _____

_____

_____

33

Monitoring Your Agency's Media Capabilities

Today's integrated marketing communications environment requires that as much attention be given to the media in which you communicate with your customers as to the messages that are delivered. Clients must work with their agencies to assure that they are receiving the best media thinking possible. At the same time, an agency must constantly monitor its own media performance.

This 34-point *Media Capabilities* assessment is to be used by agency and client in evaluating the agency's media performance. The focus is on planning, buying, resources, systems, procedures, staffing, and personnel. Do you "Agree Strongly," "Agree," are "Not Sure," "Disagree," or "Disagree Strongly" with each of the following points? Circle the position that comes closest to how you feel.

AGENCY/CLIENT MEDIA RELATIONSHIPS, COMPATIBILITY, & TRUST

1. Agency management views its media department with respect and trust. AS A NS D DS

2. The client views its agency's media operation with respect and trust. AS A NS D DS

3. The client and its agency's media department work together as a team. AS A NS D DS

4. The client and agency media department have open lines of communication. AS A NS D DS

5. The client is helpful in providing all needed materials to media. AS A NS D DS

6. The media department works together as a "team." AS A NS D DS

7. Media department personnel demonstrate confidence in their abilities. AS A NS D DS

8. Media has high standards of performance. AS A NS D DS

9. Media department personnel come across as "winners." AS A NS D DS

10. The media department has strong visibility in the advertising community. AS A NS D DS

11. The media department positively promotes its accomplishments. AS A NS D DS

Monitoring Your Agency's Media Capabilities

PLANNING

1. All media options that can deliver "customer contacts" are considered. AS A NS D DS

2. The media department demonstrates a clear understanding of all pertinent aspects of the client's marketing situation. AS A NS D DS

3. Media demonstrates a clear understanding of the client's customers and customer influencers. AS A NS D DS

4. Media demonstrates a strategic planning approach rather than one guided mainly "by the numbers." AS A NS D DS

5. Media recognizes the need to establish measurable objectives. AS A NS D DS

6. Media engages in a structured preplanning activity with the client prior to the commencement of planning itself. AS A NS D DS

7. Media seeks ways in which sales promotion, direct marketing, events, public relations, etc., can be effectively integrated into the media process. AS A NS D DS

8. Media regularly develops position papers on key issues. AS A NS D DS

BUYING

1. Media buyers demonstrate a solid understanding of conditions in the marketplace that affect their negotiating ability. AS A NS D DS

2. Media buyers understand how to maximize the efficiency of a buy. AS A NS D DS

3. Media buyers understand how to develop added media effectiveness through "value-added" media buys. AS A NS D DS

4. Media buyers are skilled negotiators. AS A NS D DS

5. Media buyers show an ability to adequately forecast future media costs and audience delivery. AS A NS D DS

RESOURCES, SYSTEMS, & PROCEDURES

1. The media department recognizes the need for research to measure results. AS A NS D DS

2. Media demonstrates the use of innovative, creative approaches to media research and assessing customer media preferences. AS A NS D DS

3. The media department has adequate media research resource material. AS A NS D DS

4. Media utilizes up-to-date computer media research/planning systems. AS A NS D DS

5. Media utilizes up-to-date computer systems for buying, estimating, and billing/paying. AS A NS D DS

STAFFING & PERSONNEL

1. Innovative media thinking is rewarded by both the agency and client. AS A NS D DS

2. "Backroom backup" and clerical support is adequate. AS A NS D DS

3. The number of media department personnel is adequate to meet current needs. AS A NS D DS

4. The number of media department personnel is adequate to meet the needs of additional work that "should" be done. AS A NS D DS

5. The media department demonstrates initiative that extends beyond its media assignments in general. AS A NS D DS

34

107 Customer Contact Points
from A to Z

To maximize the effectiveness of your marketing communications program, reach your potential customers at the most productive times and in the most productive places. To make certain that you consider all possible communication contact points, study these locations on, in, or at which you could reach your customers. Check those where you might make contact, and then investigate what vehicles you can use to reach your prospects at these locations. While these are only a fraction of the places at which to make customer contact, they will start you thinking!

	Good Contact Point
Airplane	☐
Airport	☐
Amusement park	☐
Audiotape	☐
Auto dealership	☐
Auto repair shop	☐
Auditorium	☐
Balloons	☐
Bar or tavern	☐
Bathroom	☐
Beach	☐
Bike path	☐
Boat	☐
Bowling alley	☐
Bus	☐
Bus shelter	☐
Calendar	☐
Car	☐
Car rental agency	☐

107 Customer Contact Points from A to Z

	Good Contact Point
Car wash	☐
Casino	☐
Catalog	☐
CD	☐
Church	☐
Circus	☐
Clock	☐
Clothing	☐
Computer	☐
Conference	☐
Convention	☐
Coupon	☐
Daycare center	☐
Dentist's office	☐
Doctor's office	☐
Drug store	☐
Elevator	☐
Entrance (to someplace)	☐
Exit (from someplace)	☐
Fair	☐
Fax machine	☐
Flea market	☐
Gallery	☐
Gas station	☐
Golf course	☐

107 Customer Contact Points from A to Z

	Good Contact Point
Grocery store	☐
Health club	☐
Home shopping	☐
Hospital	☐
Hotel	☐
Hotel room	☐
Jogging path	☐
Kiosk	☐
Laundromat	☐
License plate	☐
Magazine	☐
Mail	☐
Mall	☐
Military base	☐
Motel	☐
Motel room	☐
Museum	☐
Newspaper	☐
Newspaper stand	☐
Nursing home	☐
Office	☐
Package	☐
Parade	☐
Park	☐
Phone booth	☐

107 Customer Contact Points from A to Z

Good Contact Point

Playground	☐
Program	☐
Race car	☐
Radio	☐
Resort	☐
Restaurant	☐
Retirement community	☐
Road	☐
Roadside stand	☐
School	☐
Ski hill	☐
Sports event	☐
Stadium	☐
Store	☐
Street corner	☐
Swimming pool	☐
Synagogue	☐
Taxi	☐
Telephone	☐
Television	☐
Theater	☐
Toll booth	☐
Trade show	☐
Train	☐
Train station	☐

107 Customer Contact Points from A to Z

Good Contact Point

Travel agency	☐
Truck	☐
Truck stop	☐
Video arcade	☐
Video game	☐
Videos	☐
Waiting room	☐
Wall	☐
Window	☐
Xmas tree	☐
Yard	☐
Yellow Pages	☐
Zoo	☐
_____	☐
_____	☐
_____	☐

35

The Media Value Checklist

Every medium has certain distinct characteristics that contribute to (or detract from) the effective and efficient communication of advertising to the consumer. Noted in *The Media Value Checklist* is whether each of these characteristics tends to be a positive or a negative force. In the adjacent boxes, check those points that are of significance to you. The results of your media appraisal will help you determine whether or not a given medium should be included in your media mix. With the increasing focus on new, nontraditional media, use this same evaluation technique in determining their value in your marketing communications programs.

	+ Force	- Force	Significance to Me
TELEVISION			
Intrusive	X		☐
Impactful with sight, sound, movement	X		☐
Highly merchandiseable to the trade	X		☐
National-network and local-spot flexibility	X		☐
Sponsorship/program control potential	X		☐
Immediate broad reach potential across many target audiences	X		☐
High frequency potential in selected dayparts (day, late night)	X		☐
Opportunities to flight or pulse in line with budget and product potential	X		☐
Increasing concern with clutter and zapping		X	☐
High absolute costs for network		X	☐
Subject to sudden price escalation due to laws of supply and demand		X	☐
A mass medium with less-efficient delivery against narrowly defined targets		X	☐
Short-term delivery risk due to continuous programming changes		X	☐
High costs of commercial production		X	☐

The Media Value Checklist

	+ Force	– Force	Significance to Me
CABLE TELEVISION			
Highly selective programming to zero-in on highly selective target audiences	X		☐
Sponsorship opportunities to achieve program identity	X		☐
Upscale audiences with higher incomes, more education, and larger families	X		☐
Product exclusivity	X		☐
Ability to test creative commercial ideas at low media costs	X		☐
Flexible commercial message lengths and forms	X		☐
National-network and local-spot flexibility	X		☐
Ability to tag commercials locally on some networks	X		☐
Low costs per commercial announcement	X		☐
Excellent CPMs for network cable	X		☐
Ability to build high frequency of exposure	X		☐
Opportunity to compensate for lower broadcast ratings in cable homes	X		☐
Less than full national reach with cable coverage in two-thirds of all U. S. homes		X	☐
Coverage deficiencies in certain markets		X	☐
Local cable buys generally expensive with high CPMs		X	☐
Proof-of-performance problems		X	☐
Less research than on broadcast television		X	☐

The Media Value Checklist

	+ Force	- Force	Significance to Me
RADIO			
National-network and local-spot flexibility	X		☐
"Theater of the Mind" using listener's imagination	X		☐
Wide variety of formats and personalities for targeted exposure to specific demographic segments	X		☐
Enhances a television campaign with audio "imagery transfer"	X		☐
Strong merchandising from networks and local stations	X		☐
Significant local market identification	X		☐
Ability to build high frequency of exposure	X		☐
Good reach potential through multiple station buys	X		☐
Reaches mobile audience often at point nearest purchase	X		☐
High summer listening when TV viewing is lowest	X		☐
Low costs per commercial announcement	X		☐
Excellent CPMs	X		☐
Often used as a background medium for other activities		X	☐
Limited to single audio dimension		X	☐
Clutter with as many as 18 commercial minutes per hour		X	☐
High cost for broad reach due to audience fragmentation		X	☐
30-second commercials priced expensively relative to 60s		X	☐
A need for high repetition to communicate		X	☐

The Media Value Checklist

	+ Force	- Force	Significance to Me
MAGAZINES			
Significant audience selectivity against various demographic and psychographic groups	X		☐
Compatible and product-enhancing editorial environment	X		☐
Long life with opportunity for repeat exposure	X		☐
Opportunity for longer reader exposure to ad message	X		☐
Excellent color reproduction	X		☐
Creative opportunities with a variety of different space units	X		☐
Wide geographic and demographic flexibility	X		☐
Broad reach potential through use of large circulation magazines and/or a variety of different category books	X		☐
Strong reach among upscale targets	X		☐
Builds audience among light TV viewers	X		☐
Good overall CPMs when pass-along audience is included	X		☐
Excellent efficiencies relative to other media among very selective, upscale targets	X		☐
Nonintrusive relative to broadcast because reader self-selects subject matter		X	☐
Growing clutter in ad banks and low editorial ratios in certain magazines		X	☐
Single visual dimension only		X	☐
Moderate to low frequency builder		X	☐
Generally below-average delivery in the South and parts of the West (partly a function of demographics in these areas)		X	☐
Continuing question of print communication value relative to television		X	☐
High regional and metro rate premiums		X	☐
Uncertainties created with rate negotiating		X	☐

The Media Value Checklist

	+ Force	– Force	Significance to Me
NEWSPAPERS			
Immediate, announcement value in newsworthy environment	X		☐
Benefits from established reader habits	X		☐
Opportunity for long copy, shopping perusal	X		☐
Special-interest targeting potential in specific sections and papers (college, ethnic)	X		☐
Geographic targeting	X		☐
Merchandiseable to local dealers	X		☐
High local market penetration and identity	X		☐
Growing variety of space units	X		☐
Strong coop opportunities, with local retail support	X		☐
Short lifespan, with little repeat exposure opportunities		X	☐
Retail ad clutter with little competitive separation		X	☐
Predominantly primary readership with limited secondary or pass-along readers		X	☐
Unreliable (but improving) ROP color reproduction		X	☐
Declining readership among younger adults and in suburban areas		X	☐
High cost of running multimarket campaign		X	☐
High CPMs except for small space units		X	☐
Difficult to attain true national coverage due to concentration in major urban areas		X	☐
Mass penetration allows little audience selectivity		X	☐
Limited negotiability		X	☐
Premiums for special positions		X	☐
Significant premiums for national vs. local advertisers		X	☐

The Media Value Checklist

	+ Force	- Force	Significance to Me
SUNDAY SUPPLEMENTS			
High local market coverage due to newspaper carrier penetration	X		☐
In-home, relaxed readership	X		☐
Good color reproduction	X		☐
Highly merchandiseable	X		☐
Broad reach potential	X		☐
Local market impact with a magazine format	X		☐
Little secondary or pass-along audience		X	☐
Not a considered purchase, like magazines		X	☐
Limited audience selectivity due to means of distribution		X	☐
High out-of-pocket cost and CPM for national coverage		X	☐
OUT-OF-HOME			
Excellent reminder medium supporting other vehicles	X		☐
24-hour exposure	X		☐
Opportunity for strong package and product identification	X		☐
Graphic flexibility	X		☐
Strong local market presence	X		☐
Broad reach and high frequency potential	X		☐
Impact of large space units	X		☐
Opportunity to rotate locations to maximize audience delivery	X		☐
Positioning opportunities near the point of purchase	X		☐
Excellent CPMs	X		☐
Limited to short, simple message		X	☐

The Media Value Checklist

	+ Force	- Force	Significance to Me
Demographic selectivity difficult, although not impossible		X	☐
Increasingly restricted availabilities due to zoning laws		X	☐
High out-of-pocket costs for multimarket coverage		X	☐

DIRECT MAIL

	+ Force	- Force	Significance to Me
High degree of demographic, geographic, and "buying behavior" selectivity depending upon mailing list used	X		☐
Wide variety of sizes, shapes, and forms	X		☐
Intrusive	X		☐
Numerous response options	X		☐
Flexible	X		☐
Excellent reproduction	X		☐
High reach potential against selected targets	X		☐
Ability to build frequency through multiple mailings	X		☐
Timing not subject to media availability	X		☐
Reaches target at home or at work	X		☐
Efficient if target is hard to reach with mass media	X		☐
Not a requested or purchased medium by the consumer and must stand on its own for recognition		X	☐
Often regarded as "junk mail"		X	☐
A short life, unless of real interest to the consumer		X	☐
High cost and CPM for mass distribution		X	☐
Impacted by postal regulations		X	☐

The Media Value Checklist

	+ Force	- Force	Significance to Me
YELLOW PAGES			
Wide availability	X		☐
Long life span	X		☐
High use among consumers	X		☐
Reaches consumers who want to buy	X		☐
Directs consumers to purchase locations	X		☐
A medium sought out by consumers	X		☐
Geographically targeted	X		☐
Developing new products like Audiotex	X		☐
Developing directories targeted to ethnic and special-interest groups	X		☐
Low advertising production costs	X		☐
Fragmentation of market with multiple directories		X	☐
Lack of immediacy		X	☐
Relative lack of flexibility		X	☐
Long lead times		X	☐
Clutter		X	☐
Not viewed as a creative medium		X	☐
High costs for multiple directory buys		X	☐
Limited once-a-year frequency		X	☐

36

20 Points for Assessing the Value of Place-Based Media

Place-based media have positioned themselves as a means of contacting the consumer at the best possible time in the best possible location to maximize a brand's marketing communications impact. Today, place-based media vehicles are found in stores, doctor's offices, airports, restaurants, and at most other locations where people gather.

Every place-based media option should be evaluated within the context of a product or service's overall marketing communications network. Use the following place-based media values checklist to determine how well a specific opportunity will communicate with your customers and whether it will be superior to, merely equal to, or less effective than other available options.

1. It targets consumers in nontraditional places.

   This value is important to me and this place-based media option will _____

   _____ .

2. It targets consumers in locations where the product can be purchased.

   This value is important to me and this place-based media option will _____

   _____ .

3. It targets consumers where the product purchase can be influenced.

   This value is important to me and this place-based media option will _____

   _____ .

4. It showcases a product in relevant areas.

   This value is important to me and this place-based media option will _____

   _____ .

5. It minimizes nonprospect waste.

   This value is important to me and this place-based media option will _____

   _____ .

6. It hits active people on the go.

   This value is important to me and this place-based media option will _____

   _____ .

20 Points for Assessing the Value of Place-Based Media

7. It targets consumers who will respond to specific products and messages.

   This value is important to me and this place-based media option will _____
   _____ .

8. It can distinguish a brand from others in the category.

   This value is important to me and this place-based media option will _____
   _____ .

9. It allows a marketer to control the consumer's demographics, psychographics, and buying behavior based upon the message delivery location.

   This value is important to me and this place-based media option will _____
   _____ .

10. It targets active buyers rather than passive viewers or readers.

    This value is important to me and this place-based media option will _____
    _____ .

11. With in-store options, it can act as an extension of the manufacturer's sales force—a personal sales enhancement.

    This value is important to me and this place-based media option will _____
    _____ .

12. Being at the right time and place, it can be an effective "trigger to action."

    This value is important to me and this place-based media option will _____
    _____ .

13. It can be effectively targeted to very specific local market conditions.

    This value is important to me and this place-based media option will _____
    _____ .

20 Points for Assessing the Value of Place-Based Media

14. Unlike traditional media, which are often looked at as an interruption, place-based media can target people seeking interruptions from boredom.

    This value is important to me and this place-based media option will _____

    _____ .

15. It delivers a "surprise exposure."

    This value is important to me and this place-based media option will _____

    _____ .

16. It meets a specific target consumer in a place where this consumer is likely to be found and where the product may seem desirable or necessary.

    This value is important to me and this place-based media option will _____

    _____ .

17. It can increase the frequency of unplanned product purchases.

    This value is important to me and this place-based media option will _____

    _____ .

18. It can enhance a consumer benefit in the consumer's mind.

    This value is important to me and this place-based media option will _____

    _____ .

19. It may be difficult for the consumer to ignore it.

    This value is important to me and this place-based media option will _____

    _____ .

20. It will not reach the consumer too late after he or she has already made a purchase decision.

    This value is important to me and this place-based media option will _____

    _____ .

Implementing
a Media Buy

The implementation of a sound media buy should follow a well-organized, step-by-step procedure.

First, you must examine your overall media communications requirements as documented in the media plan. These will help you determine how well each media opportunity can accomplish your objectives.

Next, you will evaluate and negotiate specific media proposals.

In the third stage, a decision to buy is made. That is the time to send out order letters, handle the trafficking of advertising materials, and wrap up all publicity and promotion efforts surrounding the purchase.

After the buy has been made and the advertising begins to run, you will evaluate audience response, prepare stewardship reports, and handle billing and payment. At the same time, you will continue to explore future media opportunities.

Implementing a Media Buy is shown below in a flow chart.

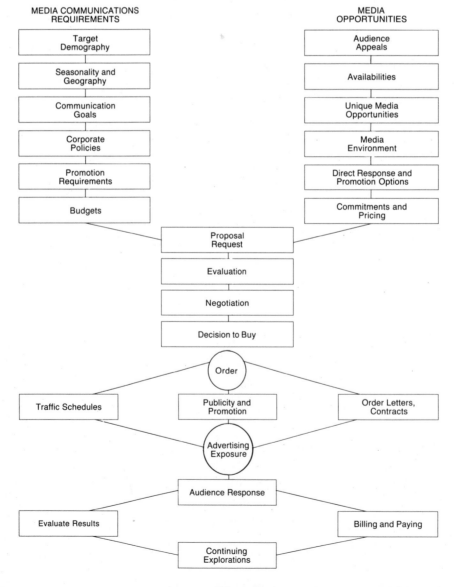

35 Value-Added Media Opportunities

Media have significantly extended their sales strategies to offer a wide variety of value-added marketing programs. A truly effective, value-added program must help the marketer to better reach and influence the consumer. It must also be well integrated into the company's overall marketing communications effort.

A company should not simply accept whatever value-added programs are offered by a medium. It should specifically indicate to the medium what value-added activities can most effectively enhance its marketing efforts. Study the following 35 value-added opportunities. Check those that would be an effective addition to your marketing communications program and initiate discussions with the media as to how they might make them available to you.

	An Effective Value-Added Addition
African-American programs	☐
Asian-American programs	☐
Barter opportunities	☐
Bonus pages or spots	☐
Cause marketing programs	☐
College programs	☐
Contests	☐
Corporate multimedia programs	☐
Couponing opportunities	☐
Custom publishing	☐
Custom research	☐
Custom videos	☐
Database programs	☐
Event marketing	☐
Free-standing inserts	☐
Gay market programs	☐
Hispanic programs	☐
In-store promotions	☐

35 Value-Added Media Opportunities

An Effective Value-Added Addition

Kid programs ☐

Mall tours ☐

Mature market programs ☐

Music promotions ☐

Place-based media opportunities ☐

Product placement in movies ☐

Product sampling ☐

Speakers ☐

Special sponsorships ☐

Spokesperson talent availability ☐

Sports sponsorships ☐

Sweepstakes ☐

Tickets ☐

Talent for sales meetings ☐

Theme park activities ☐

Trade marketing opportunities ☐

Trade show participation ☐

_____ ☐

_____ ☐

_____ ☐

39

Guiding the Search
for a Creative Media Concept

In an ever-changing advertising environment, marketers must constantly seek out new ways to reach their customers with maximum communications effectiveness. Using this creative media concept questionnaire as a guide, ask yourself each of the following questions. Your answers will help you explore new media options as you develop future advertising plans and media strategies.

1. How can a creative concept in one medium "precondition" an audience to receive a message that follows it in another medium in order that this latter exposure can work harder? (Example: A magazine or newspaper ad that promotes your new television infomercial.)

_____

_____

2. How can a creative media concept provide a synergistic editorial and advertising bond, help to attract the consumer to your message, and even hold the reader's eyes on your message for important added seconds? (Example: An ad for baby food placed next to an editorial feature on caring for infants.)

_____

_____

3. How can a creative media concept deliver multiple exposures of a single insertion at no added cost? (Example: An ad continued from one page to the next that results in the reader flipping back and forth to get the full effect of the message.)

_____

_____

4. How can a creative media concept deliver a dominant presence in a medium and position a company or brand as dominant in the industry? (Example: A "live" outdoor billboard in front of which performers demonstrate a product.)

_____

_____

5. How can a creative media concept deliver the impact of a larger space unit, but at less cost than for the larger unit? (Example: A "checkerboard" magazine spread with editorial material interspersed between the advertising.)

_____

_____

The Search for a Creative Media Concept

6. How can a single "blockbuster" creative media concept set you apart from the competition? (Example: A "pop-up" magazine ad.)

_____

_____

7. How can a creative media concept make the consumer actually seek out your advertising? (Example: Delivering a crossword puzzle to the consumer as part of your ad.)

_____

_____

8. How can a creative media concept add believability and authenticity to a product or brand story? (Example: A television commercial for a new fast-start lawn mower in which the mower is actually started live on television.)

_____

_____

9. How can a single creative media concept provide the sole basis for a brand or company's advertising effort and provide exceptional public relations "topspin"? (Example: A music video created by an advertiser that incorporates the product into the message and is run on MTV.)

_____

_____

10. How can a creative media concept deliver a sales promotion effort in a new or unique environment? (Example: A video or an audio "coupon" in which the commercial tells the viewers or listeners how they can make their own money-saving coupon.)

_____

_____

11. How can a creative media concept deliver a message that is too involved, complex, or unusual to deliver through traditional media channels? (Example: A video designed to show the product or service in an environment that will encourage viewing.)

_____

_____

12. How can a creative media concept be delivered to the consumer when he or she is shopping or participating in an activity related to your product? (Example: Advertising on shopping bags.)

_____

_____

13. How can a creative media concept provide you with exposure in an environment where your competition dominates everything around you? (Example: "Sponsoring" the sports scores in the newspaper if your competition actually sponsors all of the sports on television.)

_____

_____

14. Anything else?

_____

_____

The Creative Media Pocket Planner

A portable organizer designed to stimulate innovation and the development of creative media ideas in and out of meetings...on airplanes and commuter trains...at the beach or out in the yard...anywhere by anyone at anytime.

The Product or Service

1. What customer response do I want my marketing communications program to produce?

_____

_____

_____

2. What traditional media approaches can help deliver this response?

_____

_____

_____

3. What media will my customers expect me to use?

_____

_____

_____

4. What media do I expect my competition to use?

_____

_____

_____

5. What seems to be missing from my media plan?

_____

_____

_____

6. What creative media concepts can I relate to my customers and...

Who they are? _____

_____

How they use my product or service? _____

_____

Where they use it? _____

_____

When they use it? _____

_____

7. What unique media twist that I have always wanted to try might work?

_____

_____

_____

8. Could I create a media blockbuster and extend it over time and across different media?

_____

_____

_____

SAMPLE CREATIVE MEDIA IDEA STARTERS

- ☐ Roadblocking (commercials opposite each other)
- ☐ Gridlocking (commercials opposite, before, and after each other)
- ☐ Program sponsorship
- ☐ Announcing one media event in another medium
- ☐ Season, day, or time tie-ins
- ☐ Multiple messages in a row (the Burma Shave Effect)
- ☐ Matched multimedia synergy (business magazines plus business television)
- ☐ The live event
- ☐ Readership-enhancing editorial adjacencies
- ☐ Related program environment (the Weather Channel and snow tires)
- ☐ Infomercials
- ☐ Polling with the telephone
- ☐ MiniQuiz (commercials between question and answer)
- ☐ Cross-media promotions
- ☐ Commercial tags with offers
- ☐ Multiple small space ads
- ☐ New magazine premiere issues
- ☐ Exclusive magazine special-issue sponsorships
- ☐ Sponsored videocassettes
- ☐ Product videos (also MTV music videos)
- ☐ Pop-up ads
- ☐ Electronic talking and flashing ads
- ☐ Scented ads
- ☐ Unusual sizes and shapes
- ☐ Tie-ins with major events
- ☐ Tie-ins with natural phenomena
- ☐ Public relations tie-ins
- ☐ Direct marketing tie-ins
- ☐ Computer diskettes
- ☐ CDs

41 How to Evaluate TV Special Sponsorship Opportunities

To stand out in an increasingly cluttered advertising environment, companies may seek opportunities in television program sponsorship. Because high risks and large dollar commitments are associated with sponsoring a television special, a decision to sponsor must be carefully considered. This checklist will guide you in evaluating sponsorship opportunities in light of a company's overall marketing and advertising objectives.

	YES	NO

1. Will the special reach your target audience? ☐ ☐

   Why not? _____

   _____

2. Will the program content be compatible with your overall marketing communications objectives and corporate policies? ☐ ☐

   Why not? _____

   _____

3. Will the program environment enhance the delivery of your corporate and/or product commercials? ☐ ☐

   Why not? _____

   _____

4. Does it have the potential to deliver an audience size commensurate with the cost of sponsorship? ☐ ☐

   Why not? _____

   _____

5. Can it be regarded as a major television event that will truly stand out from regular television programming? ☐ ☐

   Why not? _____

   _____

6. Can it be effectively promoted to potential viewers and to the trade? ☐ ☐

   Why not? _____

   _____

	YES	NO

7. Can you benefit from being in a sheltered or controlled environment away from your competition and other advertisers?   ☐   ☐

Why not? _____

_____

8. Is the program idea fresh, innovative, and different? Will it let you stand out from the crowd of other advertisers?   ☐   ☐

Why not? _____

_____

9. Do the production staff and talent have strong credentials?   ☐   ☐

Why not? _____

_____

10. Will all aspects of the show be handled with good taste?   ☐   ☐

Why not? _____

_____

11. Does the special have the potential to generate strong, positive publicity and earn awards?   ☐   ☐

Why not? _____

_____

12. Can you anticipate receiving strong, positive viewer response?   ☐   ☐

Why not? _____

_____

13. Are there merchandising and promotion opportunities that can be easily, effectively, and efficiently exploited?   ☐   ☐

Why not? _____

_____

TV Sponsorship Opportunities

	YES	NO

14. Can you benefit from utilizing variable-length commercials, including 90-second and 2-minute messages? ☐ ☐

Why not? _____

_____

15. Will you have flexibility in what you choose to say in the opening and closing billboards? ☐ ☐

Why not? _____

_____

16. Does the special have long-term "evergreen" potential? Could you be associated with it annually? ☐ ☐

Why not? _____

_____

17. Will the special serve as a focal point for a thematically integrated marketing communications effort? ☐ ☐

Why not? _____

_____

18. Is the special the best of potential alternatives? ☐ ☐

Why not? _____

_____

19. Will your investment in a special be more productive than spending the same dollars on other marketing activities? ☐ ☐

Why not? _____

_____

Questions to Ask When Considering Sponsorship of an Event

A growing number of advertisers have shifted traditional media dollars into event marketing. Used properly, the sponsorship of an event can have a very positive effect on your customers, the trade, and your own employees. Its value can even extend to influencing educators, community leaders, government, and many other publics. The event must "pay out" for you, however. Consider the 18 points on this checklist when evaluating an event marketing program.

	YES	NO
1. Will the event relate to your product or service's communications and selling strategies?	☐	☐

Why not? _____

_____

_____

| 2. Will it be integrated into your company's overall marketing efforts? | ☐ | ☐ |

Why not? _____

_____

_____

| 3. Is the sponsorship tied into a major promotion? Will it provide a "hook" for a more effective promotion? | ☐ | ☐ |

Why not? _____

_____

_____

| 4. Can the event also generate added trade and sales force support and enthusiasm? | ☐ | ☐ |

Why not? _____

_____

_____

Considering Sponsorship of an Event

5. Will the event attract interest among your prime prospects, or among a segment of potential prospects or purchase influencers otherwise hard to reach?   ☐   ☐

Why not? _____

_____

_____

6. Does the event have a reasonable chance of being a "hit"? Is it a fresh idea, or is it old and tired?   ☐   ☐

Why not? _____

_____

_____

7. Does the event offer strong public relations values?   ☐   ☐

Why not? _____

_____

_____

8. Will the event offer you extended promotion opportunities over time, and from year to year?   ☐   ☐

Why not? _____

_____

_____

9. Will the sponsorship provide you with an extensive presence at the event itself? With on-site signage? Company identification on the participants themselves? Products on-site?   ☐   ☐

Why not? _____

_____

_____

Considering Sponsorship of an Event

	YES	NO

10. Will the event be broadcast on radio, TV, cable so that advertising can be tied to the sponsorship?   ☐ ☐

    Why not? _____

    _____

    _____

11. Can the impact of your sponsorship be enhanced by related paid media advertising?   ☐ ☐

    Why not? _____

    _____

    _____

12. Will you be able to tie in local events with a major national event?   ☐ ☐

    Why not? _____

    _____

    _____

13. Would the dollars accomplish more if you simply spent additional money on media advertising?   ☐ ☐

    Why not? _____

    _____

    _____

14. Will the event let you stand out from your competition?   ☐ ☐

    Why not? _____

    _____

    _____

15. Will you be able to get along well with "partners" who co-sponsor the event?   ☐ ☐

    Why not? _____

    _____

    _____

Considering Sponsorship of an Event

	YES	NO

16. If you decide to bow out of the sponsorship after a few years, will you be able to do so without any embarrassing publicity in the media? ☐ ☐

Why not? _____

_____

_____

17. Can the event succeed for you without excessive time and effort by your staff? ☐ ☐

Why not? _____

_____

_____

18. Do you have a plan for evaluating the event's performance? ☐ ☐

Why not? _____

_____

_____

Methods for Evaluating Event Sponsorship

    I. Media Coverage

        A. Amount of Coverage

        B. Type of Coverage

            1. Prospect targeted vs. general audience
            2. Visibility of company identity in coverage

    II. Pre- and Post-Sponsorship Surveys

        A. Sponsor and/or Product Recall

        B. Attitude Change

        C. Image

    III. Actual Response Delivered

        A. Leads

        B. Sales

        C. Trade Support

43

How to Evaluate a New Media Opportunity

Hardly a week goes by that marketers are not presented with at least one new media opportunity for consideration. Regardless of whether it is a new magazine, a new cable network, or any other new audience delivery system, 11 very basic questions must be answered in determining whether it can be an effective part of your marketing communications program.

	YES	NO
1. Will it fill a consumer need or niche better than an already existing vehicle?	☐	☐
2. Will it entice potential readers, listeners, or viewers to want to spend money on it or time with it?	☐	☐
3. Could a competitor come along and do a better job with a similar vehicle?	☐	☐
4. Is there a large enough potential audience to financially support it?	☐	☐
5. Will its audience match that of my target prospects and will it appeal to them?	☐	☐
6. Do the backers of the new media vehicle have the financial support and the skills needed to make it a success?	☐	☐
7. Will its introduction be supported with a very strong promotional effort?	☐	☐
8. Will advertising in this new media vehicle be priced competitively to other media opportunities?	☐	☐
9. Is there a value in my becoming a charter advertiser in this new vehicle?	☐	☐
10. Will advertising in this new vehicle give me a real edge over my competition?	☐	☐
11. Will it effectively fit into my integrated marketing communications program?	☐	☐

11 Keys to the Success of a New Information Delivery System

Much attention is being focused on the development of new information delivery systems, many of them computer based. In determining whether or not one of these systems can efficiently and effectively communicate with your customers, answer each of the following 11 questions. In every case, compare the new system to an existing customer contact system you are currently using.

	YES	NO
1. It offers more useful information to my potential customers.	☐	☐
2. It is faster for the customer to use.	☐	☐
3. It is easier for the customer to use.	☐	☐
4. It is less expensive for the customer to use.	☐	☐
5. It reaches more potential customers.	☐	☐
6. It reaches more of my *better* customers.	☐	☐
7. It can create more customer excitement and greater customer response.	☐	☐
8. It is more economical for me to use than another system.	☐	☐
9. It creates an "edge" for me vis-à-vis my competition.	☐	☐
10. It is not just a "short-term" novelty. Rather, it will have "long-term" value in terms of reaching my customers.	☐	☐
11. It is worth my time and effort to get involved with it.	☐	☐

Two-Way Interactivity: 11 Insights

The two most important communications developments impacting on the consumer in the 1980s and early 1990s were cable television and the VCR. Cable provided viewers with a greater choice of what to view. The VCR coupled this with a new freedom to choose when to view. As we move closer to the year 2000, the focus is on two-way interactivity. Whether it is delivered by computer, by cable, by the telephone company, or by a combination of these systems, "passive viewers" become "active participants" in a whole range of activities. *Two-Way Interactivity: 11 Insights* will help you determine the role that interactivity can play in your marketing communications activities.

1. Interactivity can deliver a highly targeted, personal message to my different customers.

   This is important to me because _____

   _____

2. Interactivity will let my customers talk back to me.

   This is important to me because _____

   _____

3. Interactivity will let my customers talk to each other.

   This is important to me because _____

   _____

4. Interactivity will let my customers order something immediately from me.

   This is important to me because _____

   _____

5. Interactivity can let me establish a "store" in the homes of consumers who live in areas where I don't have stores.

   This is important to me because _____

   _____

6. Interactivity can let me get immediate feedback from my customers and potential customers on all kinds of subjects.

   This is important to me because _____

   _____

7. Interactivity can let stockholders all across the country participate in our annual meeting from their own homes.

   This is important to me because _____

   _____

8. Interactivity will let me test a new product idea with consumers before I spend lots of money manufacturing the product.

   This is important to me because _____

   _____

9. Interactivity can expand the number of services I offer my customers.

   This is important to me because _____

   _____

10. Interactivity will let me establish a much closer, long-term relationship with my customers.

   This is important to me because _____

   _____

11. Interactivity will give me an edge over my competition.

   This is important to me because _____

   _____

Reaching Consumers in a High-Tech Environment: 12 Facts of Life

Hardly a week goes by without some announcement of a major strategic alliance among computer, telephone, and cable companies, the movie studios, and the media conglomerates to develop new communications delivery systems of all sizes and shapes. "Superhighways" of 500 or more channels of information and entertainment will come into our homes, much of it on demand and interactive.

Whether you are eyeing one of these developments as an investor or as a marketer, deciding whether it offers an effective new way to deliver contacts with the consumer, never forget these following 12 facts of life.

1. The consumer is not interested in high-tech delivery per se.

2. The consumer will elect to use only what is relevant to his or her needs.

3. The consumer must be reached on his or her own terms, where and when he or she wishes to be reached.

4. The consumer does not care whether the telephone company or the cable company controls the information superhighways that come into his or her home.

5. The consumer DOES care what travels down these superhighways.

6. The consumer will need help in learning how to access the information and entertainment that comes into his or her home.

7. The consumer will be naturally attracted to information and entertainment on demand because the media at last will fit his or her schedule.

8. The consumer will welcome home shopping with open arms if the promise is delivered and the price is right.

9. The consumer will decide if and when to be "interactive."

10. The consumer will judge the fate of every new communications option based on its ease of use, savings of time or money, and delivery of results.

11. The consumer will have an acceptable brand set of delivery systems just as he or she has an acceptable set of brand products at the supermarket.

12. The consumer will not care when a program is broadcast, except for very special events.

A Guide to 19 Key Media Terms

Although media strategies must be developed on the basis of qualitative as well as quantitative factors, many media decisions will always be based upon numbers. This guide defines and provides appropriate examples and equations for 19 of the most important media concepts.

For the sake of simplicity, the examples provided generally refer to demographic audience breakdowns for television and magazines. The basic concepts still apply to all media, and the target and media descriptions can be in terms of psychographic, lifestyle, or buying behavior as long as the data needed for the analyses are available.

MEDIA, MEDIUM, MEDIA VEHICLE

Magazines, television, radio, newspapers, the Yellow Pages, direct mail, etc. are together referred to as the *media*. Magazines or television alone is each a *medium*. The specific magazine *Good News* and the television show *All About Ron* are each a *media vehicle*.

DEMOGRAPHICS

Any breakdown of a population, a group of prospects, or a media audience by such characteristics as age, income, education, family size, etc.

Key Note: Demographics can be poor predictors of consumer behavior. Prospects may be better described in terms of their lifestyle, their psychographics, or their product consumption. It is frequently difficult, however, to define media audiences in terms of these same psychographic, lifestyle, or product usage characteristics.

AUDIENCE

The number or percent of persons or homes reading, listening to, or viewing a particular media vehicle. When expressed as a percent, it refers to the audience coverage of a media vehicle.

Key Note: The audience of a media vehicle can be based upon any demographic, psychographic, lifestyle, or product usage group.

Example: An issue of *Good News* reaches 18,000,000 adults, 10% of all adults in the country. It reaches 260,000 adults who regard themselves as Eternal Optimists, 20% of all Eternal Optimists.

$$\text{Coverage} = \frac{\text{Media Audience (numbers)}}{\text{Universe Population (numbers)}} = \frac{260,000}{1,300,000} = 20\%$$

RATING

The percent of people or homes reached by a single issue of a publication or episode of a program. A rating is a measure of audience size.

Key Note: The "base" of a rating is <u>all</u> homes or <u>all</u> people in a *given* demographic group. When expressed in numbers of homes or people rather than as a percent, ratings are referred to as *impressions*.

Example: Of all adult women in the country, 16% watched *All About Ron* at 8 PM last Thursday night. This represented 15,200,000 of the 95,000,000 women.

AUDIENCE COMPOSITION

The demographic makeup of the audience of a media vehicle or schedule.

Example: Of all persons reading *Good News*, 50% are women; 30% are men; 9% are teens; and 11% are children under 12.

COVERAGE VS. COMPOSITION

Coverage (or penetration) is a *percent of all people in a demographic group* exposed to a media vehicle or media schedule. Composition is a *percent of a media vehicle or schedule's total audience* that falls within this demographic group.

Key Note: Because it is a percent *of the total number of persons in a group,* coverage is an "absolute number." Composition is a "relative" number or a measure of "selectivity." Media vehicles with small numbers of readers, viewers, or listeners often sell themselves on the basis of their audience composition or "selectivity." Large mass media vehicles more often sell themselves on the basis of their (vast) audience coverage.

Example:

Demographic Universe:		Audience of Good News		
Group	Population	Readers	Coverage[1]	Composition[2]
A	40,000,000	4,000,000	10%	22%
B	30,000,000	4,500,000	15	25
C	45,000,000	2,700,000	6	15
D	15,000,000	4,800,000	32	27
E	50,000,000	2,000,000	4	11
TOTAL	180,000,000	18,000,000	10%	100%

1. Read across. 2. Read down.

HOMES USING TV (HUT)— PEOPLE USING TV (PUT)

The percent of homes or people who are watching television at a given time regardless of what they are viewing.

Key Note: The base of HUT or PUT is all homes or people in a given demographic group or geographic area regardless of whether their TV set is on or not.

Example: At 8 PM on a Thursday night in February, 64% of all women in the country were watching television.

SHARE OF AUDIENCE

The percent of those homes or people using television at a given time who are tuned to a particular program.

Key Note: The base of a share is only those homes or people in a given demographic group *who have their TV sets on.*

Example: Those 16% of all women watching *All About Ron* at 8 PM on Thursday night represented 25% (the share) of 64% of all women viewing something on television at that time.

Rating = Homes (or People) Using TV × Share of Audience

$$\text{Share} = \frac{\text{Rating}}{\text{Homes (or People) Using TV}}$$

$$\textit{All About Ron's } 25\% \text{ (Share)} = \frac{16\% \text{ (Rating)}}{64\% \text{ (Women Using TV)}}$$

GROSS RATING POINTS (GRPs)

The total number of rating points (against a specific demographic group) for a particular media schedule.

Key Note: Target Rating Points (TRPs) is the term often used when referring to ratings based upon a specific target audience of people rather than upon homes.

GRPs = Sum of All Ratings in a Schedule

GRPs = Average Rating × Number of Commercials or Insertions

GRPs = Reach × Frequency

Example:

	A Schedule in Five Magazines		
	Number of	Average Rating	
Magazine	Insertions	Men	Women
A	2	10	20
B	1	8	6
C	3	4	10
D	4	12	8
E	2	6	6
Total Schedule	12	100 GRPs	120 GRPs

REACH

The number or percent of *different* homes or people in a specified demographic group who are exposed one or more times to a schedule of media vehicles.

Key Note: It is necessary to use tables and computer programs based upon patterns of audience accumulation and duplication to estimate the reach for various media schedules.

Example: The preceding magazine schedule delivered 100 GRPs against men. It is estimated that this schedule would reach 50% of all men at least once.

DUPLICATION

The number of people exposed to more than one of a group of media vehicles.

Example: The portion of viewers of *All About Ron* and the readers of *Good News* who *both* see the TV show and read the magazine.

COMBINED (OR RANDOM) REACH OF TWO MEDIA

A simple equation used to determine the reach of two different media if the reach of each medium is known. First, add together the reach of medium A and the reach of medium B. Then, subtract from this an estimate of the duplication between the two schedules (A × B).

$$\text{Combined Reach} = (A + B) - (A \times B)$$

Example: A magazine schedule reaches 70% and a television schedule reaches 50% of all college graduates in the country. The combined reach of the two schedules is:

$$\text{Combined Reach} = (70\% + 50\%) - (70\% \times 50\%) = 120\% - 35\% = 85\%$$

Key Note: A third medium is added by using the random reach of 85% as A and the third medium's reach as B. The equation can be extended in the same manner to additional media.

AVERAGE FREQUENCY

The number of exposures received by the average home or person reached by a media schedule. This may include several exposures to the same media vehicle or exposures to several different media vehicles.

Key Note: Reach, frequency, and GRPs are all interrelated.

$$\text{Reach} \times \text{Frequency} = \text{GRPs}$$

$$\text{Frequency} = \frac{\text{GRPs}}{\text{Reach}}$$

$$\text{Reach} = \frac{\text{GRPs}}{\text{Frequency}}$$

Example: The 100 men GRP magazine schedule reached 50% of all men at least once. The average man reached was exposed to the schedule twice.

$$\text{Frequency} = \frac{\text{GRPs}}{\text{Reach}} = \frac{100}{50} = 2.0$$

EFFECTIVE FREQUENCY

The minimum number of times (frequency) an advertiser feels its message must be exposed to a consumer to positively impact on that consumer's awareness, attitudes, sales intent, or other behavior with regard to the product or service.

Key Note: A schedule's mathematical frequency distribution is easily calculated through a number of computer-based media planning systems. The decision as to exactly how many exposures are needed, however, is a judgment call. It depends upon the marketing, creative, and media elements involving the specific product or service.

VIEWERS PER VIEWING HOME (VPVH)

The average number of persons viewing a program in each viewing home.

Example: *All About Ron* is being viewed in 19,000,000 homes by 15,200,000 women. This is an average of 0.8 women viewers per home.

$$\text{VPVH} = \frac{\text{Total Viewers}}{\text{Total Viewing Homes}} = \frac{15,200,000}{19,000,000} = 0.8$$

Key Note: Because less than a "whole" woman cannot view a show, this is now referred to as Viewers per 1,000 or Viewers per 100 Viewing Homes. In the case of *All About Ron*, there would be 800 women viewers per 1,000 viewing homes.

CIRCULATION

The total number of copies of a publication sold or otherwise distributed through all channels of distribution.

Example: The circulation of *Good News* magazine is 3,600,000.

READERS PER COPY

The average number of people that a single copy of a publication reaches.

Example: *Good News* magazine has 5.0 adult readers per copy.

$$RPC = \frac{\text{Magazine Readers (Audience)}}{\text{Magazine Circulation (Copies)}} = \frac{18,000,000}{3,600,000} = 5.0$$

PRIMARY AUDIENCE READERS, SECONDARY OR PASS-ALONG AUDIENCE READERS

A publication's primary readers include only those persons who subscribe to a publication, buy a single copy, or read a copy purchased by someone with whom they live. Secondary or pass-along readers are everyone else exposed to an issue of a publication regardless of how or where they come in contact with it. A publication's total audience is the sum of both groups of readers.

Example: Of the 18,000,000 *Good News* readers, 6,000,000 are primary readers and 12,000,000 are secondary or pass-along readers.

COST PER THOUSAND

The media cost to deliver 1,000 impressions (or bodies) within a specifically defined demographic group. CPMs are used to compare efficiencies of different media vehicles or media schedules.

Example: A page four-color ad in *Good News* costs $54,000. Because it is read by 18,000,000 adults, its cost per thousand for adults is $3.00.

$$CPM = \frac{\text{Cost}}{\text{Audience (000)}} = \frac{\$54,000}{18,000} = \$3.00$$

Customer Contact Reach Calculator

An integrated marketing communications program focuses on effectively reaching and touching the consumer through a variety of contact points. It considers traditional as well as nontraditional activities involving advertising, events, sales promotion, public relations, direct marketing, product exposure, etc.

The *Customer Contact Reach Calculator* helps you estimate the combined reach of multiple contact activities if you know the reach of each individual activity. For example, assume that your television plan reaches 50% of your target audience, a special event reaches 10%, and a sampling program reaches 20% of your prospects. At the point where the reach of the TV plan and special event intersect, you'll find that together they reach 55% of your prospects. At that point where their combined reach and the reach of the sampling program (20%) intersect, you will find the reach is now up to 63%.

Contact Medium One

%	5	10	15	20	25	30	35	40	45	50	55	60	65	70	75	80	85	90	95
5	10	14	19	24	29	33	38	43	48	52	57	62	66	71	76	81	85	90	95
10	14	19	23	28	32	37	41	46	50	55	59	63	68	72	77	81	86	90	95
15	19	23	28	32	36	40	44	48	53	57	61	65	69	73	78	82	86	90	95
25	29	32	36	40	43	47	50	54	58	61	65	69	72	76	79	83	87	90	95
30	33	37	40	43	47	50	53	57	60	64	67	70	74	77	80	84	87	90	95
35	38	41	44	47	50	53	57	60	63	66	69	72	75	78	81	84	87	90	95
40	43	46	48	51	54	57	60	62	65	68	71	74	76	79	82	85	88	90	95
45	48	50	53	55	58	60	63	65	68	70	73	75	78	80	83	85	88	90	95
50	52	55	57	59	61	64	66	68	70	73	75	77	79	82	84	86	88	91	95
55	57	59	61	63	65	67	69	71	73	75	77	79	81	83	85	87	89	91	95
60	62	63	65	67	69	70	72	74	75	77	79	80	82	84	86	87	89	91	95
65	66	68	69	71	72	74	75	76	78	79	81	82	84	85	86	88	89	91	95
70	71	72	73	75	76	77	78	79	80	82	83	84	85	86	87	88	90	91	95
75	76	77	78	79	79	80	81	82	83	84	85	86	86	87	88	89	90	91	95
80	81	81	82	82	83	84	84	85	85	86	87	87	88	88	89	90	90	91	95
85	85	86	86	86	87	87	87	88	88	88	89	89	89	90	90	90	91	91	95
90	90	90	90	90	90	90	90	90	90	91	91	91	91	91	91	91	91	91	95
95	95	95	95	95	95	95	95	95	95	95	95	95	95	95	95	95	95	95	95

Contact Medium Two

Part IV

Public Relations, Publicity, and Promotions

Properly implemented, public relations is a very effective marketing communications tool. It can publicize a business, its products, and its services. It can enhance the value of a business's many different activities and efforts. And it can be used to deal with outside influences—government actions, the consumer, or competition—that impact upon it. Public relations activities involve many different avenues of exposure. The key to its most effective implementation is knowing how appropriate each activity is under different sets of circumstances. In other words, you need to know what works best...and when. Part IV will help you find out.

49. 20 Public Relations, Publicity, and Promotional Ideas
50. A 17-Point Press Release Checklist
51. 6 Guidelines for Responding to a Threatened Boycott

20 Public Relations, Publicity, and Promotional Ideas

Many public relations activities can enhance a company's marketing activities and its position in the minds of its many publics. The key is knowing which activities work best and under what conditions. At J. Walter Thompson Co., and as an independent consultant, Sheryl Johnston has been counseling clients on the effective use of public relations for more than 20 years. This checklist of *20 Public Relations, Publicity, and Promotional Ideas* can help you choose the right public relations tool at the right time. As Sheryl says, "The main problem people have with public relations is that they should not use it when they honestly have nothing to say!"

Public Relations Activity	Appropriate for	Not Appropriate for
1. PRESS RELEASE—a news story that relates the who-what-when-why-where to the media.	Announcing news about a company, product, idea, promotion, person, or event.	Situations when there is no story to tell (e.g., a product sampling event only).
2. PRESS KIT—Generally includes more than one news release, sometimes a fact sheet, photographs, biographical information, etc.	A story that requires in-depth understanding from the media.	A story that is already familiar or is of little significance.
3. POSTERS, BROCHURES, SIGNAGE—Posters announcing an event or idea; brochures providing consumer information; signage designed to attract attention.	Posters and signs should be used when the purpose is to attract attention without going into a great deal of detail. Brochures work best when they can be easily distributed free of charge (e.g., at an event, through a P.O. box, in an editorial or broadcast placement, or on a package offer).	Posters and signs should not be used when message is too complex, or requires a lot of detail. Situations in which what the brochure has to say is not really useful.

Public Relations and Promotional Ideas

Public Relations Activity	Appropriate for	Not Appropriate for
4. PROMOTIONAL GIMMICK —a gift or gimmick that is provided to the media or consumers, in addition to the story.	A situation in which the gimmick is intended to amuse or attract attention, or remind the recipient of a story or event.	A story of a serious nature.
5. MAT RELEASE—is a black and white story and sometimes photo that can be reproduced in sizes from a column to a full page. It generally contains product or client mention and is usually run as is by editors of suburban and smaller newspapers. Client pays for production and distribution.	A story that doesn't require in-depth analysis. Good for questions and answers, recipes, contest announcements, trivia quizzes, basic who-what-when-why-where news stories.	A story that requires the editor's opinion or analysis. A story that could easily get picked up on its own because of its significance.
6. ROP COLOR PAGE—A mat feature that generally includes a color photo, recipes or "how to" tips, and a story. Client or agency provides the copy, recipes, and photo. ROP service takes care of layout, production, and distribution to editors. The editor will generally use as is, with a limited amount of commercial mentions, and can choose to use his/her own byline. If copy is too commercial, they will drop out brand name. ROP color pages usually are a half to a full page and run on the front cover of the newspaper food or lifestyle section. Cost is paid for totally by client, or can be shared with another sponsor. (Typical joint sponsors would be a barbecue sauce and a barbecue grill, or a food product with a drink.)	Recipe stories on new or existing products. Feature stories with recipes or tips, brochure send-away offers. "How to" stories affecting meal preparation or lifestyles.	A story that requires no visual and would be easily picked up by editors as a straight news release. A story that doesn't relate to food or lifestyles.

Public Relations and Promotional Ideas

Public Relations Activity	Appropriate for	Not Appropriate for
7. PRINT CONTEST—might be a recipe or essay contest in which you provide a magazine or newspaper with the editorial idea and the prize package. In exchange, they give you space and mention of the object of your promotion. (Note: Not the same as a paid space sweepstakes.)	Promoting a special event, theme, product, etc.	Situations where there is no natural editorial tie-in, or the subject is of interest to a small group of people (unless you are going to a special-interest publication that is only reaching one particular audience).
8. RADIO TRADE FOR MENTION CONTEST—a radio promotion in which the client or agency offers a prize package (such as an all-expenses-paid trip, product, cash, or various other items) to a station in "exchange for mention." The rule of thumb: The contest should have listener appeal. The station should provide client with a total number of mentions equal (in air time) to the value of the prize package.	Promoting a special event, name, or product.	Promoting an idea or product that has serious overtones (e.g., a piece of medical equipment, a life-threatening situation). A story or prize package that would only be of interest to a small group of people.
9. PUBLIC SERVICE ANNOUNCEMENT (PSA)— an announcement that is intended to educate or benefit the consumer audience (with no commercial mentions). These may be electronically produced or submitted in written form to be read by a station announcer. They generally come in 20-, 30-, and 60-second formats (check with station for requirements). Nonprofit status is usually required.	Educational message such as health or safety information. Event announcement (as long as it is for nonprofit reasons).	Brand name announcement. (Example: You could submit a PSA from the American Dairy Association about the benefits of cheese. But you couldn't submit a PSA for the benefits of Kraft cheese.)

Public Relations and Promotional Ideas

Public Relations Activity	Appropriate for	Not Appropriate for
10. AN AUDIO NEWS RELEASE OR PAID, SYNDICATED RADIO INTERVIEW—Again, a consumer interest news story. This would be distributed to radio stations for use during various parts of the day. Client pays for production and distribution.	A consumer news interest story. Note: Must be logged by the radio station as "news" or "public affairs" programming.	A totally commercial message. A piece of news that has no benefit to the audience.
11. A VIDEO NEWS RELEASE —a news feature that tells a short story about an issue or product that affects consumers in some way. This is distributed to television news outlets and sometimes talk shows for use on-air, as is. The client pays for the production and distribution.	A trends story. A consumer-interest story that can be told in a noncommercial way. Note: Think of it as being part of a newscast.	A totally commercial message. A piece of news that has no benefit to the audience.
12. MEDIA SPOKESPERSON TOUR—Offering a media spokesperson to promote your product or idea to the general public. Usually consists of a combination of print or broadcast interviews and sometimes personal appearances.	Presenting a new product or idea to the general public. Promoting a personality such as a performer, politician, author, or athlete. Crisis public relations situation (something has happened that has in some way had a negative effect on the general public). Offering send-away (how-to or informational) brochures.	Any story that is of interest to a small group of people only. Any story that is too commercial. It should, in some way, benefit the viewing, reading, or listening audience. Couponing (with no story to tell).

Public Relations and Promotional Ideas

Public Relations Activity	Appropriate for	Not Appropriate for
13. PRESS CONFERENCE—an event to which a selected group of media is invited to hear an announcement or watch a demonstration of major significance. (Note: In general, the media resists press conferences if they can obtain the news another way. They will only attend if a major personality is announcing something or if a major issue is to be discussed.)	A major announcement that has an effect on, or would be of interest to, consumers.	An announcement that has a small effect. Just meeting someone (with no major announcement).
14. SATELLITE MEDIA TOUR OR PRESS CONFERENCE —This kind of event is becoming increasingly popular because it saves wear and tear on a media spokesperson and is often more cost-effective. Your spokesperson is brought into a TV studio in a major city for a day or two to conduct interviews with news and talk show personalities in other cities via satellite. Stations are notified in advance of this opportunity and can request a hook-up and specific interview time. The advantage for them is that it makes their viewing audience think that they are on the scene, providing news coverage as it happens. The benefit for you or your client is that you've achieved maximum exposure over a very short period of time.	A story of national or broad regional interest. Promoting a product, idea or event. Communicating a point of view, particularly in a situation of crisis or controversy.	A local story. Any story that is too commercial—it should be newsworthy.

Public Relations and Promotional Ideas

Public Relations Activity	Appropriate for	Not Appropriate for
15. SCHOOL PROMOTIONS—Teachers and students can be an important audience when the message is educational. Typical kinds of activities include study guides, posters or brochures, contests that will benefit the learning process.	Promotion of a program, event, or idea that has educational value.	Situations in which youth is not an important target audience, or if message is too commercial and has no educational purpose.
16. PROCLAMATION OR OFFICIAL MESSAGE—A presidential, mayoral, or other governmental message or proclamation is used to give special designation to an idea that affects the public. Example: "Country Music Month," "National Heart Week," "Black History Month," etc.	Giving special recognition to an idea or event.	Promoting a product or commercial message. Promoting an idea that is only of interest to a select or small group of people.
17. ENDORSEMENTS—have been around for years, but in today's issue-oriented environment, they are more important than ever. Recommendations are sought from groups with a public interest (particularly in the areas of environment, wildlife, education, health, etc.). If you can add "endorsed by" or "recommended by" a prestigious organization to your press materials, it adds credibility and weight to your image and attracts public attention.	A story that is issue-oriented and in some way affects or benefits the general public.	A story that only benefits a very small group of people or an isolated segment of society. A story that is lighthearted, self-serving or commercial.

Public Relations and Promotional Ideas

Public Relations Activity	Appropriate for	Not Appropriate for
18. OUTSIDE CONSULTANTS/ SPECIALIZED SERVICES— are used on a regular basis in today's economics-conscious environment. Public relations agencies and other businesses are hiring experts on a permanent or freelance basis to help plan strategy, attract media attention, and add credibility to their marketing campaigns. There is a growing need for consultants in areas that affect our nation's future, such as healthcare, public safety, the environment, high technology, etc. Lobbyists are also being employed to bring about legislation that will affect specific industries.	Issue-oriented news stories. Preventing a crisis or controversy. Once a crisis has occurred, as a restorative measure.	Stories that do not affect the health, education, safety, and general well-being of the public.
19. EXHIBIT SPACE—a space in which you exhibit or distribute a product (or information).	New product introduction. New ways of using a product. Distributing information. Giving presentations or demonstrations.	Distributing very dry information. Exhibiting an existing product with nothing new to show or tell.
20. SAMPLING EVENT—an event in which the client offers its product to the public. Sometimes includes the distribution of a coupon and/or brochure, in addition to product sample.	Encouraging trial and usage of new or existing product. Presenting an existing product in a new way, or to secure new audiences.	Media coverage (unless there is something highly unusual going on).

50

A 17-Point
Press Release Checklist

The managing director of RECOGNITION/Public Relations Pty Limited in Australia reports that "whenever I am stuck for ideas in some marketing situation, I know I'll find a solution within a few minutes of picking up *Advertising & Marketing Checklists*."

Their 17-Point Press Release Checklist will help others around the world to maximize the effectiveness of marketing communications efforts.

1. Is it news?

   Is this something that's new and different? Have we made it clear? Why would a journalist want to use it?

2. What are the benefits?

   Present the news in terms of the benefits it will bring to readers.

3. Does it reveal trends?

   Rather than give isolated details, reveal the trends, causes, and effects behind the details. Will this release help readers make sense of the world?

4. Is the opening right?

   Journalists don't have time to waste. Grab their interest with the headline (maximum 15 words) and back it up in the first paragraph (maximum 20 words). Avoid funny/clever headlines.

5. What's our target?

   Large, computerized mailings can be disappointing. Every release should be targeted to a specific publication. Each publication has its own well-defined requirements. What suits one won't suit another. If we try to please everyone, we'll please no one.

6. Are we having a rave?

   No self-respecting journalist is going to run an article that describes a product as "a revolutionary advance that's light-years ahead of its competitors!" Stick to the facts. When giving an opinion, give it as a quote.

7. Any jargon?

   Don't assume your reader is going to understand technical jargon.

8. Is it relevant to *your* country?

   Don't pass on press releases from a foreign head office. Rewrite overseas releases so they fit your country's style and include comments from the chief in your country.

9. Is it written from the customer's point of view?

    Prospective customers love to read what their competitors are doing. Write up news of a contract from the customer's point of view. For example, "Smith Engineering buys Arco motors," will interest more prospects than, "Arco sells motors to engineering group."

10. Are we fitting in with deadlines?

    Look at each publication's deadline before sending out media releases. A magazine with a six-week lead time may be reluctant to run a piece if the dailies run it first.

11. Is it easy to use?

    Double space, have big margins. Apply the dozen or so rules that produce clear writing.

12. Have we introduced a personality?

    People like to read about other people. Have plenty of quotes. Quote people the way they talk—don't make them sound like a legal document.

13. How good are the photos?

    Photos have to *look* interesting. This often requires a lot of thought and effort. Supply artwork such as graphs and diagrams whenever possible.

14. Facts checked?

    Check facts carefully (again). People take delight in pointing out errors to journalists.

15. Is it the right length?

    Don't pad it out, but don't make it too short. Length is determined by asking, "Are we providing all the facts the journalist is likely to need?" If it's a long release, break it up into modules.

16. After-hours numbers?

    Journalists are likely to want extra information outside normal hours. Make sure you give them an after-hours contact.

17. Has it been approved?

    Always get the final version, photo, and caption approved by the client and any third party.

51

6 Guidelines for Responding to a Threatened Boycott

In recent years, advertisers have received an increasing number of threats of consumer boycotts from activist groups opposed to television programs and/or magazines that they claimed contained excessive sex or violence. When threatened with a boycott, you will in most cases respond in writing to the group opposing the media environment in which your advertising appears. Refer to the following six guidelines and make certain to consult with your public relations counsel in drafting your response.

1. Avoid being on the defensive, apologizing, saying it was a mistake, or indicating it will never happen again.

2. Explain it has never been your company's policy to influence a medium's editorial or programming content.

3. Indicate that in a democracy, the consumer should determine the success or failure of a medium. That he or she should decide what to read, listen to, or view...just as he or she should be free to decide for whom to vote, how to pray, where to shop, etc.

4. Comment that the program in which your commercials appeared was reviewed prior to airing and that the subject matter was felt to have been handled in good taste.

5. Emphasize that your company runs advertising in many different media vehicles that effectively reach your customers and that your advertising schedule is never meant as an endorsement or rejection of a medium's position or policies.

6. State that in a free society, a company should not be threatened for its legal exercise of the right of free speech.

Part V

Targeting and Selling through Direct Marketing

Specialized catalogs...home-shopping shows...interactive television...data bases that focus on the best prospects for every conceivable product and service. These are just a few of the reasons why direct marketing is the fastest-growing field in advertising. Today, every medium is benefiting from direct marketing as advertisers seek new ways to target their prime customers and communicate with them more effectively and efficiently. The eight checklists and charts in Part V will help you determine whether direct marketing is right for your business—and how you can reap its many benefits.

52. When to Use Direct Marketing

53. Bob Stone's Tips for Direct Marketing Success (Abridged)

54. A Guide to Profitable & Productive Business-to-Business Telemarketing

55. Guidelines to Effective Frequency-Marketing Programs

56. A Final Checkup for Effective Catalog Copy

57. Art or Photography in Catalogs: Which Way Should You Go?

58. "Golden Rules" for 800-Number Success

59. 12 Keys to the Effective Use of Direct Marketing Order Forms

125

52

When to Use Direct Marketing

The 1980s produced an explosion in direct marketing that is growing far faster than general advertising. It has attracted many marketers who had never previously considered using it as part of their marketing communications mix. Is direct marketing right for you? Ask yourself the following 19 questions. If you answer "Yes" to any one of them, indicate below the question where and how you could put it to work for you.

Is This Important to You?

	YES	NO

1. When the product or service requires a full explanation and you must communicate a message that is too complex or detailed to be conveyed in general advertising. ☐ ☐

   _____

   _____

2. When it is a unique product or service for which other distribution channels are either not available, too expensive, or otherwise unsatisfactory. ☐ ☐

   _____

   _____

3. When you must produce an immediate *and* identifiable order or inquiry. ☐ ☐

   _____

   _____

4. When a specific, selected market of prime prospects is both definable and recognizable and where lists or media vehicles are available to target them. ☐ ☐

   _____

   _____

5. When a specific, selected market or target audience is desired and other media can deliver it only with excessive waste circulation. ☐ ☐

   _____

   _____

When to Use Direct Marketing

	YES	NO
6. When a personal, personalized, or confidential communication is desired.	☐	☐
7. When the marketing strategy calls for a format that cannot be carried in a general media buy.	☐	☐
8. When a specific market needs to be covered with a minimum of spillover into adjacent areas.	☐	☐
9. When sampling is practical and highly desirable.	☐	☐
10. When precise timing or frequency of contact is needed.	☐	☐
11. When it is desirable to conduct research to measure effectiveness within certain markets; determine prospect profiles; or test price, packaging, or potential users within a market.	☐	☐
12. When a highly controlled distribution is required.	☐	☐

When to Use Direct Marketing

	YES	NO

13. When the sale of the product directly to the prospect, without dealers or retailers, is desired. ☐ ☐

_____

_____

14. When you want to secure leads that will be followed up by personal sales contacts or further direct mail. ☐ ☐

_____

_____

15. When you want to direct a specific prospect to a specific location. ☐ ☐

_____

_____

16. When you want to introduce your product or service to potential prospects in a highly personal manner. ☐ ☐

_____

_____

17. When you want to build and refine mailing lists. ☐ ☐

_____

_____

18. When you want to follow up inquiries secured through other media vehicles, including responses to sales promotion offers. ☐ ☐

_____

_____

19. When you want to turn the "short-term" response to a sales promotion offer into a "long-term" customer relationship and capitalize on the lifetime potential value of that customer. ☐ ☐

_____

_____

53

Bob Stone's Tips for Direct Marketing Success (Abridged)

The success of a direct marketing effort is spelled P-L-A-N-N-I-N-G! It depends upon myriad factors, including the product or service, the media, the offer, the communications format, the preliminary testing, and a thorough analysis of the results. In his book *Successful Direct Marketing Methods*, Bob Stone zeros in on what makes a direct marketing effort successful. Focus on each of these tips as you plan and implement your direct marketing effort. If your efforts need improvement, use the available space to suggest new action.

The Product or Service

	YES	NO
1. Is it a real value for the price asked?	☐	☐

_____

_____

| 2. Does it stack up well against competition? | ☐ | ☐ |

_____

_____

| 3. Does it have exclusive features? | ☐ | ☐ |

_____

_____

| 4. Is its cost low enough to warrant a mail order markup? | ☐ | ☐ |

_____

_____

| 5. Does the product or service lend itself to repeat business? | ☐ | ☐ |

_____

_____

Bob Stone's Tips for Direct Marketing Success

The Media

	YES	NO
1. Is your customer list cleaned on a regular basis?	☐	☐

_____

_____

2. Have you developed a profile of your customers, giving you all their important demographic characteristics? ☐ ☐

_____

_____

3. Have you coded your customer list by recency of purchase? ☐ ☐

_____

_____

4. Have you worked with competent list compilers in selecting names of prospects who match the profile of those on your customer list? ☐ ☐

_____

_____

5. Have you determined how often you can successfully mail to the same list? ☐ ☐

_____

_____

6. Have you matched your offers with your markets and selected media vehicles with good direct response track records or the potential to become good direct response vehicles? ☐ ☐

_____

_____

	YES	NO

7. Have you continually monitored the true response of the media, computing for each vehicle the number of inquiries less returns, the net cash receipts, and repeat business? ☐ ☐

_____

_____

8. Have you determined the best times and the best frequency for using each media vehicle? ☐ ☐

_____

_____

The Offers

1. Are you using the most enticing offers you can within the realm of good business? ☐ ☐

_____

_____

2. Does your offer lend itself to the development of an automatic repeat business cycle? ☐ ☐

_____

_____

3. Have you determined the ideal introductory period or quantity for your plan? ☐ ☐

_____

_____

4. Have you determined the ideal introductory price for your offer? ☐ ☐

_____

_____

Bob Stone's Tips for Direct Marketing Success

The Communication Format

	YES	NO
1. Are your mailings, ads, or commercials in character with your product or service and your target market?	☐	☐

_____

_____

| 2. Does your advertising and mailing package grab attention and impel action? | ☐ | ☐ |

_____

_____

Testing

| 1. Do you consistently test the best product, media, offers, and formats? | ☐ | ☐ |

_____

_____

| 2. Have you tested the best timing and frequency of your offers? | ☐ | ☐ |

_____

_____

| 3. Do you consistently test new potential consumer markets? | ☐ | ☐ |

_____

_____

| 4. Have you determined the most responsive geographic areas? | ☐ | ☐ |

_____

_____

Bob Stone's Tips for Direct Marketing Success

Analyzing the Results

	YES	NO
1. Do you track results by source?	☐	☐

_____

_____

| 2. Do you analyze results by ZIP codes and by demographics? | ☐ | ☐ |

_____

_____

| 3. Do you compute the level of repeat business by original source? | ☐ | ☐ |

_____

_____

Source: *Successful Direct Marketing Methods,* 5th edition, by Bob Stone (1994).

54

A Guide to Profitable & Productive Business-to-Business Telemarketing

A skilled business-to-business telemarketer understands his or her prospects, has a solid knowledge of the product or service he or she represents, and knows precisely how to talk convincingly on the phone in order to elicit a positive response. As the head of her very successful telemarketing business, Kathy Kaatz McRae has developed this *Guide to Profitable & Productive Business-to-Business Telemarketing*.

A successful telemarketing program accomplishes six goals:

1. It targets "qualified" prospects to minimize waste.

2. It provides the marketer with a better understanding of the prospect's wants and requirements.

3. It builds long-term relationships with prospective customers.

4. It sets "confirmed" appointments.

5. It presells prospects to make the follow-up appointments more efficient.

6. It sells!

Successful telemarketing callers have six personality characteristics:

1. They have strong communication skills.

2. They are assertive.

3. They are articulate.

4. They are intuitive.

5. They are well organized.

6. They are friendly.

Profitable & Productive Business-to-Business Telemarketing

Successful telemarketing callers:

1. Never pre-judge a prospect.

2. Carefully and quickly qualify a prospect.

3. Never waste time with prospects who fail to qualify or have no purchasing power.

4. Invest in good, clean lists to minimize rejections.

5. Fully understand, but do not memorize, the material they will discuss with the prospect.

6. Personalize every call.

7. Respect each prospect and the value of his or her time.

8. Are good note takers, taking down names, titles, referrals, best times to call, personal information, etc.

9. Recognize that they represent the company on behalf of whom they are calling. They never say "I" or "They," but speak of how " 'We' want this opportunity to . . . ."

10. View objections as opportunities rather than as stumbling blocks.

11. Understand that the harder a prospect is to reach, the fewer solicitations they will have received from competitors.

12. Never lie.

13. Constantly educate themselves about the company, the products, and the services they represent.

14. Recognize that "No!" from a prospect may not mean "No!" It might mean that this is a bad time to talk and that the telemarketer should call back later.

15. Keep a tickler file of all qualified prospects who are not ready to purchase now.

16. Recognize that changes in personnel, budgets, and time of year may alter plans—and *always* follow up.

17. Ask permission to call back.

18. Always thank the prospect for his or her time.

19. Always remember that the prospect has a life outside of his or her business.

55

Guidelines to Effective Frequency-Marketing Programs

Companies develop frequency-marketing programs to identify their best customers, and increase their long-term business with them through ongoing, value-added rewards. The most common programs involve frequent-flying, frequent-staying, and frequent-renting.

The real value of a frequency-marketing program reflects the fact that it is easier and more profitable to maintain and increase business with existing customers than to attract new customers. While there is no guarantee that a frequency-marketing program will be successful, your odds are greatly increased by following these eight guidelines.

1. An effective frequency-marketing program offers real value to the customer.

   My frequency-marketing program will do this because _____

   _____

2. An effective frequency-marketing program is easy for customers to join.

   My frequency-marketing program will do this because _____

   _____

3. An effective frequency-marketing program is easy for customers to understand.

   My frequency-marketing program will do this because _____

   _____

4. An effective frequency-marketing program will never make the customer feel that participating is more work than it is worth.

   My frequency-marketing program will do this because _____

   _____

5. An effective frequency-marketing program offers customers frequent "special bonus-participation values" to maintain their interest.

   My frequency-marketing program will do this because _____

   _____

6. An effective frequency-marketing program communicates frequently with customers and makes them feel they are important to the company.

   My frequency-marketing program will do this because _____

   _____

7. An effective frequency-marketing program recognizes that competitors may want to copy it. The company is prepared to counter these efforts.

   My frequency-marketing program will do this because _____

   _____

8. An effective frequency-marketing program can be very expensive and labor intensive to maintain. A company must be prepared to handle the administration, database maintenance, and research tracking over a long period of time.

   My frequency-marketing program will do this because _____

   _____

56

A Final Checkup for Effective Catalog Copy

A leader in catalog marketing, Maxwell Sroge has targeted eight questions marketers should ask about their copy before a catalog goes to print. Use this checklist to test your own copy, whether it is for a catalog or for general advertising. If you answer "No" to any question, analyze the problem and remedy it. It will save you time, money, and problems later on.

	YES	NO

1. Is your copy in the right, the best, and the most logical order? ☐ ☐

   Suggested Change? _____

   _____

   _____

2. Is the copy persuasive? ☐ ☐

   Suggested Change? _____

   _____

   _____

3. Is the copy complete? ☐ ☐

   Suggested Change? _____

   _____

   _____

4. Is the copy clear? ☐ ☐

   Suggested Change? _____

   _____

   _____

Checkup for Effective Catalog Copy

	YES	NO
5. Is the copy consistent?	☐	☐

Suggested Change? _____

_____

_____

| 6. Is the copy accurate? | ☐ | ☐ |

Suggested Change? _____

_____

_____

| 7. Is the copy interesting? | ☐ | ☐ |

Suggested Change? _____

_____

_____

| 8. Is the copy believable? | ☐ | ☐ |

Suggested Change? _____

_____

_____

Source: *How to Create Successful Catalogs*, by Maxwell Sroge (1995).

Art or Photography in Catalogs: Which Way Should You Go?

In his book *How to Create Successful Catalogs*, Maxwell Sroge offers this advice on the advantages of art and photography in catalog illustrations. His comments are sound whenever you must choose between art and photography in a catalog or print ad.

Which Works Best?

	Art	Photography	Combination
1. Emphasis on product function for greater customer understanding	X		
2. Easier emphasis on product detail	X		
3. Easy addition of seasonal aspects when preparing catalogs in off seasons	X		
4. Easy illustration of benefits such as bearing fruit trees	X		
5. Greater believability with the picture of the actual product		X	
6. Heightened credibility because of seeing the real thing		X	
7. Greater customer association with the product		X	
8. Emphasis on product detail with art coupled with the realism of photography			X
9. Emphasis on function			X

Source: *How to Create Successful Catalogs*, by Maxwell Sroge (1995).

11 Keys to
Home Shopping Success

The growth of home shopping has resulted in major changes in the relationship between buyers and sellers. And its importance will only increase as home shopping is coupled with interactivity, infomercials and greater channel capacity. Marketers who enter into home shopping ventures can learn much from those who have preceeded them as to what works best.

1. Home shoppers are most attracted by unique, one-of-a-kind merchandise that is not available elsewhere.

2. Since home shoppers are charged for shipping and handling, the price of the merchandise must appear to be a real bargain.

3. Make sure that what you sell looks good on TV. Whenever possible, select primary colors and avoid patterns that look fuzzy on television.

4. Fashion sellers must carry a wide selection of large sizes, since many female home shoppers wear size 14 and over.

5. Facilities *must* be adequate to handle incoming calls.

6. If your 800 number is not constantly visible, make sure it is easy to remember and displayed frequently enough for the shopper to remember.

7. Clearly explain when phone calls are taken, if it isn't 24 hours a day, 7 days a week.

8. Give the home shopper many reasons to buy what you have to sell. For example, describe how and when they might use it.

9. Look for merchandise to sell that is easy to demonstrate and has many unique features you can emphasize.

10. Your models should add glamour to your product, without overpowering it. You don't want the home shopper to say, "That won't look as good on me as it does on her!"

11. Home shoppers develop a very close rapport with the show hosts. Keep this in mind and make sure your home shoppers feel as if they are a "welcome guest in the home shopping store."

12 Keys to the Effective Use of Direct Marketing Order Forms

The last step your potential customer may take in responding to a direct marketing offer is to fill out the order form. If the form is incomplete or difficult to follow, your prospect may simply say "Forget it...I don't really want to buy this anyway!" *12 Keys to the Effective Use of Direct Marketing Order Forms* will help you keep potential prospects from becoming lost prospects.

	YES	NO
1. Keep the order form simple and neat.	☐	☐

Suggested Improvement: _____

_____

2. Make certain the spaces are large enough for the customer to fill in all the necessary information.   ☐   ☐

Suggested Improvement: _____

_____

3. Attract readers to the order form and make it easy for them to find it.   ☐   ☐

Suggested Improvement: _____

_____

4. Encourage your customers to print carefully.   ☐   ☐

Suggested Improvement: _____

_____

5. Remind them to use the mailing label if you have provided one.   ☐   ☐

Suggested Improvement: _____

_____

6. Be sure to tell customers how to pay for their orders, how much to pay including taxes and shipping, *and* where to send the order.   ☐   ☐

Suggested Improvement: _____

_____

The Effective Use of Direct Marketing Order Forms

	YES	NO

7. If you are offering an exchange or a satisfaction guarantee, explain exactly what it covers and how to take advantage of it.   ☐   ☐

   Suggested Improvement: _____

   _____

8. Let your customers build your list by asking them for the names of friends who might be good prospects.   ☐   ☐

   Suggested Improvement: _____

   _____

9. Tell your customers how long it will take for their order to be delivered.   ☐   ☐

   Suggested Improvement: _____

   _____

10. Make sure your customer knows how long the offer is good.   ☐   ☐

    Suggested Improvement: _____

    _____

11. *NEVER* print the order form white on black because your customer's writing will not show up on it!   ☐   ☐

    Suggested Improvement: _____

    _____

Part VI

Maximizing the Sales Promotion Payoff

A catalog for Toys 'Я' Us announced "Up to $491 in Coupon Savings Inside!" Coupons, contests, premiums, refunds, and samples are but a few of the techniques being used today as more dollars are shifted from image and brand-building advertising to action-oriented, short-term sales promotion. To best use sales promotion, you must determine exactly what it can and can't do for your business, decide which techniques can best accomplish your goals, and measure your results. The six checklists and charts in Part VI will guide you through these steps and help you profitably organize your sales promotion planning process.

60. The Do's and Cannot Do's of Consumer Sales Promotion

61. Consumer Sales Promotion: 41 Idea Starters

62. The Do's and Cannot Do's of Trade Sales Promotion

63. Promotion Planning Checklist

64. "Never-to-Be-Forgotten" Rules for Contests and Sweepstakes

65. Grocery Cross-Promotions: 120 Idea Starters

The Do's and Cannot Do's of Consumer Sales Promotion

During the 1980s, advertisers extensively increased their investments in sales promotion programs, both in absolute terms and often at the expense of long-term brand-building advertising. While consumer sales promotion can accomplish many objectives, there is much it cannot do. Refer to *The Do's and Cannot Do's of Consumer Sales Promotion* in determining what promotion can or cannot do for you.

Is This Important to You?

Consumer Sales Promotion *CAN*

	YES	NO
1. Reach new users.	☐	☐
2. Obtain trial for a product.	☐	☐
3. Hold onto current users of a product.	☐	☐
4. Encourage repeat usage of a product.	☐	☐
5. Build more frequent or multiple purchases of a product.	☐	☐
6. Encourage users to stock up with a big supply of a product.	☐	☐
7. Introduce a new or improved product.	☐	☐
8. Introduce new packaging or a different size package.	☐	☐
9. Neutralize competitive advertising or sales promotion.	☐	☐
10. Capitalize on seasonal, geographic, or special events.	☐	☐
11. Encourage consumers to trade up to a larger size, a more profitable line, or another product in the line.	☐	☐
12. Reinforce a brand's advertising by encouraging purchase *now*!	☐	☐

Consumer Sales Promotion

Consumer Sales Promotion *CANNOT*

	YES	NO
1. Build brand loyalty or develop a long-term consumer franchise by itself.	☐	☐
2. Reverse a declining sales trend.	☐	☐
3. Change basic consumer nonacceptance of a product.	☐	☐
4. Compensate for inadequate levels of consumer advertising.	☐	☐
5. Overcome product problems in pricing, packaging, quality, or performance.	☐	☐

Source: *Sales Promotion Management*, by Don E. Schultz and William A. Robinson (1982).

61

Consumer Sales Promotion: 41 Idea Starters

Once you decide that a consumer sales promotion program will help carry out your marketing objectives, the question becomes..."What should I do?" In developing a strategy, consider *all* options. Use this idea starter checklist by first noting techniques being used by your competitors, and then checking off programs you might consider using.

	Used by Competition	A Program We Might Use
1. Contests	☐	☐
2. Games	☐	☐
3. Instant (ruboff) sweepstakes	☐	☐
4. General sweepstakes	☐	☐
5. Prepicked winner sweepstakes	☐	☐
6. In-pack premiums	☐	☐
7. On-pack premiums	☐	☐
8. Near-pack premiums	☐	☐
9. Mail-in premiums	☐	☐
10. Self-liquidating premiums	☐	☐
11. Reusable containers	☐	☐
12. Refund on product purchase	☐	☐
13. Refund on multiple product purchase from one company	☐	☐

Consumer Sales Promotion: 41 Idea Starters

	Used by Competition	A Program We Might Use
14. Refund on related product purchase	☐	☐
15. Direct mail samples	☐	☐
16. Door-to-door samples	☐	☐
17. On-pack samples	☐	☐
18. Near-pack samples	☐	☐
19. Sample with other product purchase	☐	☐
20. Sample mail-in coupon	☐	☐
21. In-pack coupon	☐	☐
22. On-pack coupon	☐	☐
23. In-store coupon display	☐	☐
24. Cash register tape coupon	☐	☐
25. Printed shopping bag coupon	☐	☐
26. Free-standing insert coupon (FSI)	☐	☐
27. Newspaper coupon	☐	☐
28. Sunday supplement coupon	☐	☐
29. Magazine coupon	☐	☐
30. Direct mail coupon	☐	☐

Consumer Sales Promotion: 41 Idea Starters

	Used by Competition	A Program We Might Use
31. Larger size "bonus" package	☐	☐
32. Bonus unit package	☐	☐
33. Price-off label	☐	☐
34. Banded price-off pack	☐	☐
35. Trial package	☐	☐
36. Trial membership	☐	☐
37. "Buy 1...Get 1 Free"	☐	☐
38. National trading stamps (S&H)	☐	☐
39. Company's own continuity plan	☐	☐
40. Store register receipt prize plan	☐	☐
41. Frequent-buyer bonus plan	☐	☐

The Do's and Cannot Do's of Trade Sales Promotion

Just as consumer sales promotion grew extensively during the 1980s, trade promotion efforts have also sharply increased. Like consumer sales promotion, promotion to the trade can accomplish many objectives...but there is much it cannot do. Refer to *The Do's and Cannot Do's of Trade Sales Promotion* in determining what it can or cannot do for you.

Is This Important to You?

TRADE SALES PROMOTION *CAN*

	YES	NO
1. Obtain feature pricing, displays, and other dealer in-store support for a consumer sales promotion effort.	☐	☐
2. Help increase or reduce trade inventories.	☐	☐
3. Help obtain, expand, or improve product distribution.	☐	☐
4. Motivate the sales force, dealers, brokers, or wholesalers.	☐	☐
5. Improve overall trade relations.	☐	☐

TRADE SALES PROMOTION *CANNOT*

	YES	NO
1. Compensate for a poorly trained sales force.	☐	☐
2. Overcome poor product distribution.	☐	☐
3. Compensate for lack of consumer advertising.	☐	☐

Source: *Sales Promotion Management,* by Don E. Schultz and William A. Robinson (1982).

Promotion Planning Checklist

To succeed, a well-thought-out and properly implemented promotion must cover nine essential bases. Refer regularly to the *Promotion Planning Checklist* developed by two sales promotion pros, Bud Frankel, president of Frankel & Co., and Bill Robinson, president of William A. Robinson, Inc. With modifications, you can apply this checklist to many other marketing and communications situations.

Is This Base Covered?

	YES	NO
1. Market Situation	☐	☐

What is happening in the marketplace?

_____

_____

What are you doing now?

_____

_____

What is your competition doing now?

_____

_____

_____

	YES	NO
2. Problem to Be Solved	☐	☐

What is the problem?

_____

_____

What is the source of the problem?

_____

_____

Promotion Planning Checklist

3. **Sales Promotion Objectives: Measurable and Unmeasurable**   ☐   ☐

Who is the consumer target? Trade target?

_____

_____

What are you trying to motivate the target to do?

_____

_____

What markets are you talking about geographically? Demographically?

_____

_____

4. **Sales Promotion Strategies**   ☐   ☐

Do they meet the objectives?

_____

_____

5. **Sales Promotion Tactics**   ☐   ☐

Do they support the strategies?

_____

_____

Do they work?

_____

_____

Are they practical?

_____

_____

Promotion Planning Checklist

Are they measurable?

_____

_____

Are they affordable?

_____

_____

6. **Timetable**   ☐   ☐

What is the sell-in deadline?

_____

_____

How long will the promotion run?

_____

_____

What is the evaluation deadline?

_____

_____

7. **Budget**   ☐   ☐

What is the anticipated budget?

_____

_____

Is there a firmly set limit?

_____

_____

Promotion Planning Checklist

Are there any unanticipated costs that could affect the budget?

_____

_____

What is the timing of requirements for funding?

_____

_____

8. **Testing**   ☐   ☐

How will the promotion be evaluated? Through pre-testing, market test, or consumer groups?

_____

_____

What audience do you want to test with?

_____

_____

What are you looking for?

_____

_____

How will you evaluate whether to go with the promotion or not?

_____

_____

9. **Post-Promotion Evaluation**   ☐   ☐

How do you measure success?

_____

_____

Promotion Planning Checklist

Was there an increase in volume? Share?

_____

_____

What was the consumer response? The trade response?

_____

_____

How was the participation?

_____

_____

Source: "Promote," a feature of *Adweek's* "Marketing Week," April 13, 1987.

"Never-to-Be-Forgotten" Rules for Contests and Sweepstakes

Whether you are conducting a large national sweepstakes or a small local contest, its success (and often the reputation and financial well-being of your company) can depend upon how clearly the rules are spelled out. Without this, the value of the promotion can be lost amid confusion about the entry requirements, how winners are determined, and how prizes are awarded. Make certain you follow every one of these *"Never-to-Be-Forgotten" Rules for Contests and Sweepstakes* in running your promotion.

Is This Covered?

	YES	NO

REQUIREMENTS TO ENTER

1. Eligibility? ☐ ☐

   (State "Void Where Prohibited by Law")

2. Material to submit? ☐ ☐

   (State "All Entries Become the Property of _____")

3. Purchase requirements? ☐ ☐

4. Number of entries? ☐ ☐

5. Closing date of event? ☐ ☐

DETERMINATION OF THE WINNERS

1. Judging method? ☐ ☐

2. Breaking of ties? ☐ ☐

3. Judging organization? ☐ ☐

   (State "All Decisions Are Final")

Rules for Contests and Sweepstakes

AWARDING OF PRIZES

	YES	NO
1. The prize structure?	☐	☐
2. Notification of winners—when and how?	☐	☐
3. Awarding of prizes—when and how?	☐	☐
4. Providing winners' names to all interested?	☐	☐
5. Provision for unclaimed prizes?	☐	☐

Source: *Sales Promotion Management,* by Don E. Schultz and William A. Robinson (1982).

Grocery Cross-Promotions: 120 Idea Starters

With two-thirds of all grocery product purchase decisions made after the consumer enters the supermarket, it is no wonder that marketers are seeking new and innovative ways to motivate in-store purchases. High on the list are cross-promotions with related products. Unfortunately, a brand's best potential partners may be overlooked simply because you don't think of them. To help in the search, here are 120 possible partners to consider when planning grocery product cross-promotions.

Produce
Lettuce
Tomatoes
Fruit
Lemons
Limes
Melon
Herbs
Carrots
Celery
Vegetables
Cole slaw
Onions
Potatoes

Beverages
Pop
Seltzer water
Juice
Coffee
Tea
Crystal Light
Iced tea
Beer
Wine
Mixed drinks

Breads/Cereals
Wheat
White
Rye
Hamburger buns
Hotdog buns
Pita
French
Rolls
Bagels
Cereal

Dairy Case
Milk

Eggs
Cheese
Yogurt
Piecrusts
Refrigerated rolls
Cream cheese

Baby Needs
Formula
Diapers
Cereal
Jarred food

Frozen
Popsicle
Ice cream
Pizza
French fries
Dough

Chips/Crackers
Potato
Fritos
Pretzels
Salsa chips
Oyster
Crackers

Meat/Fish/Dinners
Chicken
Hamburger
Pork
Beef
Bratwurst
Italian sausage
Hotdogs
Prepared chicken entrees
Fish
Lunchmeat
Bacon
Breakfast sausage

Canned Goods
Soup
Sloppy joe
Tuna
Canned pasta
Corn
Beans
Spaghetti sauce

Dry Packaged
Pasta
Mac & cheese

Seasonings/Condiments
Mustard
Ketchup
Chili sauces
Steak sauces
Marinades
Taco seasoning
Salsa
Pickle relish
Mayo
Miracle Whip
Olives
Pickles

Treats
Cookies
Candy
Popcorn
Baking mixes
Baking ingredients

Cleaning Products
Dishwasher: Soap or detergent
SOS pads
Floors
Endust
Bathroom
Vinegar

Grocery Cross-Promotions: 120 Idea Starters

Paper Products
Napkins
Plates
Spoons, knives, forks
Cups
Bar cups
Garbage bags
Lunch bags
Kleenex
Toilet paper

Toiletries
Shampoo
Conditioner
Deodorant
Toothpaste
Contac: Aosept or saline
Tylenol
Tampax
Sanitary pads

Laundry
Detergent
Bleach
Softening sheets
Baby soap

Part VII

Researching Your Marketing Communications Activities' Health and Well-Being

Your marketing communications activities are aimed at generating a response from your customers. Sometimes the response can be measured by the ring of the cash register or the number of inquiries received. In most cases, however, the response is in terms of an intermediate measure of effectiveness, such as in awareness or attitude toward a product or service. The ten checklists and charts in Part VII will help you to better understand consumers; define the response you seek from your advertising or other marketing communications activities; evaluate research reports and research companies; develop a simple yet practical original research project; determine how much frequency is needed under varying creative, media, and marketing conditions; and more.

66. 16 Ways to Gather Consumer Insights

67. 10 Steps to Better Decisions

68. The 14-Point Advertising Response Monitor

69. An 18-Point Checkup on the Use of Research Reports

70. 11 Questions to Ask When Hiring a Research Company

71. 7 Fresh Ideas for a Simple, Homegrown Research Project

72. The Retailer's Advertising Impact Scorecard

73. How Much Frequency Is Enough?

74. Guidelines to Special Target Markets

75. Working with Numbers & Tables: 14 Tips

66

16 Ways to
Gather Consumer Insights

Marketing communications programs that fail are usually the result of a company's failure to really understand what makes the consumer tick. An effective marketing communications program begins by gathering insights into consumers' needs and desires. It must then continually monitor the attitudes and buying behavior of these consumers.

There are many ways to gather consumer insights, some as simple as observing shoppers. Indicate how each of these 16 insight-gathering ideas can be helpful to you.

A Good Idea

1. Observing shoppers ☐

   I can use this to _____

   _____

2. Special offers to customers ☐

   I can use this to _____

   _____

3. 1-800 numbers ☐

   I can use this to _____

   _____

4. Meetings with customers ☐

   I can use this to _____

   _____

5. Customer feedback panels ☐

   I can use this to _____

   _____

16 Ways to Gather Consumer Insights

A Good Idea

6. Customer warranty cards ☐

   I can use this to _____

   _____

7. Focus groups ☐

   I can use this to _____

   _____

8. Customer mail ☐

   I can use this to _____

   _____

9. Mail surveys ☐

   I can use this to _____

   _____

10. Phone surveys ☐

    I can use this to _____

    _____

11. Contests ☐

    I can use this to _____

    _____

12. In-store interviews ☐

    I can use this to _____

    _____

A Good Idea

13. Touch-screen surveys ☐

   I can use this to _____

   _____

14. Interactive computer surveys ☐

   I can use this to _____

   _____

15. Conference and convention contacts ☐

   I can use this to _____

   _____

16. Analysis of scanner data ☐

   I can use this to _____

   _____

67

10 Steps to Better Decisions

Every marketing communications decision, from defining the problem to evaluating the results, is a challenge. That's why it is essential to think before you act to insure that the decisions you make are the correct ones. *10 Steps to Better Decisions* is a process created by FIND/SVP to guide the decision-making process. FIND/SVP provides consulting by phone, delivering relevant information and answers to all sizes, shapes, and forms of client questions.

1. Look Before You Leap.

☐ What is this all about? What is the crux of the problem? What exactly needs to be decided? What is pertinent? What is the key to this situation? Is a decision really necessary?

☐ Is this problem generic or unique? Is it a symptom of a larger problem, the first occurrence of a new generic problem, or a truly exceptional event? Has a similar problem occurred before? Could this become a recurring problem? Has anyone else had this problem? Can I look to others' experience for guidance?

☐ In general, how should a decision like this be made? Is it my decision alone or should it be made in a group? Should I delegate parts of the decision? Is this primarily a "head" (analytic, sequential) or a "heart" (intuitive) decision?

☐ How long will this decision take? How much time should I expect to spend gathering information? After I gather information, will it still be difficult to make the decision? Is the deadline arbitrary or is it real?

☐ Does my definition encompass all of the known phenomena?

2. Frame the Problem.

☐ How should I decide the problem in order for my business to be successful? What are the objectives the decision must reach? What are the minimum goals it must attain? What are the conditions it must satisfy?

☐ What kind of results will give me both success and self-satisfaction? What is my definition of success? What criteria would prompt me to choose one option over another?

☐ Is my vision clearly focused on the needed results? What does my frame minimize? What does my frame emphasize? Am I considering only what meets the real need and eliminating everything else?

☐ Have I challenged my frame? Have I analyzed different frames and selected the most appropriate?

3. Know Your Blind Spots.

☐ Am I working toward my goal or just trying to avoid trouble?

☐ Do I understand my biases, assumptions, opinions, fears, limitations?

4. Shed Light on the Subject.

☐ Do I have the resources and access to information to develop a menu of options?

☐ Who has the information? What is the best way to get the information?

☐ Does this information help me discover my range of options?

5. Clarify Your Options.

☐ Can I develop several alternatives based on the information I have collected?

☐ Have I brainstormed with colleagues to ensure every reasonable option has been included?

10 Steps to Better Decisions

6. Make Judicious Use of Intuition.

☐ What is my gut reaction to each option?

☐ What would I decide if I weren't afraid?

☐ Am I thinking clearly? Do I feel stressed-out, harassed, tired, bored, distracted, depressed, confused, fatigued?

☐ Do I trust my intuition?

7. Envision the Consequences.

☐ If I choose the first option, will it give me what I need? What would happen next? What would happen two days later, two weeks later, two months later?

☐ What is the worst thing that can happen? The best thing?

☐ How clearly can I foresee the most likely results? For me? For the others involved? Does looking at past experience, others', or my own patterns, help me see ahead more clearly?

☐ Have I worked the carrying-out of the decision into the decision itself?

☐ Have I developed a second-best solution?

8. Implement the Decision.

☐ Who has to know of this decision?

☐ What action has to be taken? Who should take it? Are the people who are expected to carry out the actions capable of doing it?

9. See for Yourself.

☐ Have I seen firsthand how my decision is being carried out?

☐ Did I get feedback from the people who are affected by my decision?

☐ Have I kept records in order to keep track of the results for future reference?

☐ Are the assumptions on which I have based my decision appropriate?

10. Remain Flexible.

☐ Is the decision working out the way I'd hoped?

☐ Is there still time to modify my plan of action?

Source: FIND/SVP, 625 Avenue of the Americas, New York, NY 10011, 212-645-4500.

The 14-Point
Advertising Response Monitor

All advertising messages seek to elicit some form of human response from the consumer. This holds true whether the advertiser sells a product, a service, or an idea, and whether the consumer is a young housewife shopping for groceries or a company executive investigating new corporate benefit plans for his firm. Use *The 14-Point Advertising Response Monitor* to evaluate the performance of your advertising. In the columns to the right, indicate how well you feel your advertising is communicating. Then note in the space below how you might improve its performance.

	YES	MAYBE	NO

Was the Advertising Received?

1. Did it catch the consumer's eye? His or her ear? ☐ ☐ ☐

_____

_____

2. Did it catch his or her attention? ☐ ☐ ☐

_____

_____

3. Did it get through? ☐ ☐ ☐

_____

_____

4. Was it remembered? ☐ ☐ ☐

_____

_____

Was the Advertising Comprehended?

5. Was it understood? ☐ ☐ ☐

_____

_____

The 14-Point Advertising Response Monitor

	YES	MAYBE	NO

6. Did the consumer "get the message"?   ☐ ☐ ☐

_____

_____

7. Was the message identified with the product, the service, or the idea?   ☐ ☐ ☐

_____

_____

8. Was anything confusing or unclear?   ☐ ☐ ☐

_____

_____

Did the Advertising Make an Impression?

9. Did the consumer accept the proposition?   ☐ ☐ ☐

_____

_____

10. Did the advertising affect attitudes toward the product, the service, or the idea?   ☐ ☐ ☐

_____

_____

11. Did the consumer think or feel differently about the product, the service, or the idea after exposure?   ☐ ☐ ☐

_____

_____

The 14-Point Advertising Response Monitor

	YES	MAYBE	NO

12. Did the advertising affect perceptions of the product, the service, or the idea? ☐ ☐ ☐

_____

_____

13. Did the advertising alter perceptions of the competing products, services, or ideas? ☐ ☐ ☐

_____

_____

14. Did the consumer respond to direct action appeals? ☐ ☐ ☐

_____

_____

Source: The PACT (Positioning Advertising Copy Testing) Agencies Report (1982).

An 18-Point Checkup on the Use of Research Reports

Research is the backbone of much of the work done in advertising and public relations. While not everyone is a trained researcher, all of us should understand what constitutes good, fair, and unbiased research. Before using any research report, read the following *18-Point Checkup* to determine if it is in "good working order." First, check whether you feel each item is dealt with properly. Then, note any further information you need to determine whether or not to use the report.

	YES	NO

1. Does the report identify the organization that initiated and paid for the research? ☐ ☐

_____

_____

2. Is there a statement of the purpose of the research that clearly states what it was meant to accomplish? ☐ ☐

_____

_____

3. Are the organizations that designed and were responsible for conducting the research identified? ☐ ☐

_____

_____

4. Is there a full description, in nontechnical language, of the research design, including a definition of what is measured and how the data are collected? ☐ ☐

_____

_____

5. Is the design evenhanded; that is, is it free of leading questions and other bias; does it address questions of fact and opinion without inducing answers that unfairly benefit the study sponsors? ☐ ☐

_____

_____

Checkup on the Use of Research Reports

	YES	NO
6. Does it address questions that respondents are capable of answering?	☐	☐
7. Does the sample represent the population it is meant to represent?	☐	☐
8. Does the report specify the proportion of the designated sample from which information was collected and processed or say that the proportion cannot be determined?	☐	☐
9. Were those who collected data kept free of clues to the study sponsorship or the expected responses, or other leads or information that might condition or bias the information they obtained and recorded?	☐	☐
10. Was the sample large enough to provide stable findings?	☐	☐
11. Are sampling error limits shown, if they can be computed?	☐	☐
12. Does the report specify when the data were collected?	☐	☐

Checkup on the Use of Research Reports

	YES	NO
13. Does the report say clearly whether its findings do or do not apply beyond the direct source of the data?	☐	☐
14. If the research has limited applications, is there a statement covering who or what it represents and the times or conditions under which it applies?	☐	☐
15. Are the measurements described in simple and direct language?	☐	☐
16. Are the actual findings clearly differentiated from the interpretation of the findings?	☐	☐
17. Have all of the relevant findings been released, including all information potentially unfavorable to the sponsor or embarrassing to the responsible researcher?	☐	☐
18. Has the research been fairly presented?	☐	☐

Source: *Guidelines for the Public Use of Market and Opinion Research*, by the Advertising Research Foundation (1981).

70

11 Questions to Ask When Hiring a Research Company

At some time in your career, you may be called upon to hire a research company to conduct work for you. In deciding whom to employ, you should rely both on the recommendations of others and your own judgment. Use the following 11 questions as a guide in interviewing prospective research firms, noting any additional information you need to make an intelligent business decision.

1. Does the company have the technical competence to handle the work?

_____

_____

2. Have they demonstrated skill, common sense, and good judgment in handling other people's work and/or problems?

_____

_____

3. Will they seek imaginative and creative solutions to problems rather than simply relying upon techniques that have been used in the past?

_____

_____

4. How important will your business be to the company?

_____

_____

5. Who will be working on your business, and how comfortable do you feel with them?

_____

_____

6. How qualified is the company to analyze and summarize the research in clear, concise, and accurate terms?

_____

_____

7. Is the company familiar enough with your business to avoid making basic, logical mistakes of judgment?

_____

_____

8. Is the company honest? Will it do the kind of work that is correct rather than what it thinks you want to receive?

_____

_____

9. Will the company avoid providing you with excess "bells and whistles" that you neither want nor need? However, will it not cut corners by failing to ask enough questions or using samples that are either too small or not representative of the market you want to survey?

_____

_____

10. Can you trust the company to keep confidential the results of any work it does for you?

_____

_____

11. Is there anything about the company that concerns you that you have not asked?

_____

_____

71

7 Fresh Ideas for a Simple, Homegrown Research Project

Marketers must continually seek out new research techniques to find fresh answers to old questions. Much can be gained by simply going out and talking to people. The following ideas will suggest nontraditional, fast, and inexpensive ways of learning what your customers are thinking and doing. Be sure to note *your* ideas in the spaces provided.

	YES	NO
1. Can any research be easily done by your own staff in your own office?	☐	☐

_____

_____

_____

2. Can you quickly go to a location during lunch, over the weekend, or after work and find exactly the kinds of people to whom you want to talk?	☐	☐

_____

_____

_____

3. Will you be attending an event at which others there represent exactly the people you would like to survey?	☐	☐

_____

_____

_____

4. Would any of the media you deal with have enough interest in your project to help fund it?	☐	☐

_____

_____

_____

Ideas for a Homegrown Research Project

	YES	NO

5. Is there a college or university with whom you could work on the project? ☐ YES ☐ NO

_____

_____

_____

6. Will you be attending a conference or convention where you could slip a questionnaire under the attendees' room doors? ☐ YES ☐ NO

_____

_____

_____

7. Do you and your associates personally know key people who would answer your questions if you just asked them? ☐ YES ☐ NO

_____

_____

_____

The Retailer's Advertising Impact Scorecard

A small local retailer may try many different forms of advertising, but may not be sure what drew the most customers into his store. *The Retailer's Advertising Impact Scorecard* is a do-it-yourself survey that can help you track where your business comes from. When a customer calls or comes into the store, just ask "Would you tell me how you learned about our sale (or this new merchandise)?" or "Where have you heard about us lately?" Then check off each response on your *Scorecard*.

Check as Many Sources of Information as Appropriate

Newspapers	☐	☐	☐	☐	☐	☐	☐	☐	☐	☐	☐	☐	☐	☐	☐
Magazines	☐	☐	☐	☐	☐	☐	☐	☐	☐	☐	☐	☐	☐	☐	☐
Radio	☐	☐	☐	☐	☐	☐	☐	☐	☐	☐	☐	☐	☐	☐	☐
TV	☐	☐	☐	☐	☐	☐	☐	☐	☐	☐	☐	☐	☐	☐	☐
Cable	☐	☐	☐	☐	☐	☐	☐	☐	☐	☐	☐	☐	☐	☐	☐
Direct Mail	☐	☐	☐	☐	☐	☐	☐	☐	☐	☐	☐	☐	☐	☐	☐
In-Store Signs and Promotions	☐	☐	☐	☐	☐	☐	☐	☐	☐	☐	☐	☐	☐	☐	☐
Yellow Pages	☐	☐	☐	☐	☐	☐	☐	☐	☐	☐	☐	☐	☐	☐	☐
Outdoor Boards	☐	☐	☐	☐	☐	☐	☐	☐	☐	☐	☐	☐	☐	☐	☐
Window Displays	☐	☐	☐	☐	☐	☐	☐	☐	☐	☐	☐	☐	☐	☐	☐
Word-of-Mouth	☐	☐	☐	☐	☐	☐	☐	☐	☐	☐	☐	☐	☐	☐	☐
_____	☐	☐	☐	☐	☐	☐	☐	☐	☐	☐	☐	☐	☐	☐	☐
_____	☐	☐	☐	☐	☐	☐	☐	☐	☐	☐	☐	☐	☐	☐	☐
_____	☐	☐	☐	☐	☐	☐	☐	☐	☐	☐	☐	☐	☐	☐	☐
_____	☐	☐	☐	☐	☐	☐	☐	☐	☐	☐	☐	☐	☐	☐	☐
_____	☐	☐	☐	☐	☐	☐	☐	☐	☐	☐	☐	☐	☐	☐	☐
_____	☐	☐	☐	☐	☐	☐	☐	☐	☐	☐	☐	☐	☐	☐	☐

How Much Frequency Is Enough?

"How much frequency is enough?" While there is no one answer to this question, with too little repetition an ad may have little impact on the consumer. With excessive repetition, an ad can lose its ability to effectively communicate, persuade, or create positive attitudes.

The following checklist can guide you in determining frequency. Examine the 21 message, media, and market-related factors and check the boxes that apply to you. Then analyze your competition in the same manner. (The overall scoring of attributes is highly subjective.) The goal is to see the degree to which the "more" factors outweigh the "less" factors in your specific case...*and* to determine whether you may need more or less frequency than your competition.

When You Need MORE Frequency　　　　　　　**When You Need LESS Frequency**

Message Factors

When You Need MORE Frequency			When You Need LESS Frequency
New advertising campaign	☐	☐	Older advertising campaign
Many different themes	☐	☐	A single theme
Complicated message	☐	☐	Simple message
Long message	☐	☐	Short message
Small size	☐	☐	Large size
Low-keyed, nonabrasive	☐	☐	Intrusive
Similar to competition	☐	☐	Different from competition
General image advertising	☐	☐	Specific product sell
Nonemotional content	☐	☐	Highly emotional message

Media Factors

When You Need MORE Frequency			When You Need LESS Frequency
Exposure in few media	☐	☐	Exposure in many media
Flighted schedule	☐	☐	Continuity schedule
Highly cluttered environment	☐	☐	Uncluttered environment
Noncompatible environment	☐	☐	Compatible editorial setting
Low attention-holding media	☐	☐	High attention-holding media

How Much Frequency Is Enough?

When You Need MORE Frequency			When You Need LESS Frequency
Market Factors			
Infrequently purchased product	☐	☐	Frequently purchased product
Low-interest product	☐	☐	High-interest product
New product	☐	☐	Established product
Strong competition	☐	☐	Limited competition
A minor brand in category	☐	☐	A major brand in category
Infrequently used product	☐	☐	Frequently used product
Limited promotional activity	☐	☐	High promotional activity

☐ **The Overall Frequency Skew** ☐

74

Guidelines to
Special Target Markets

Hardly a week goes by that there is not a new report on the growing importance of one or more segments of the population. Whether they are children, older adults, Hispanics, African-Americans, gays, college students, sports buffs, or any other special group, companies increasingly want to reach and influence them with new integrated marketing communications programs.

As you study the behavior and lifestyle characteristics of a market, you must determine *why* they are special and *why* they require special attention. You next must determine the most effective and innovative ways to reach and touch them. By answering the following ten questions, you will be able to more clearly analyze special target markets.

1. What is the definition of the special market?

   _____

   _____

2. How did the special market develop over time?

   _____

   _____

3. What makes the market so special?

   _____

   _____

4. How much is the special market worth overall in sales potential?

   _____

   _____

5. How much is the special market worth to you specifically?

   _____

   _____

6. Why does the market deserve special attention? What are the rewards of focusing special attention on the market? What are the penalties of not doing so?

_____

_____

7. How does the special market differ from the population in general and/or from other markets in terms of demographics, behavior, lifestyle, product interests, buying habits, media habits, etc.?

_____

_____

8. What companies should be especially interested in the market?

_____

_____

9. Where does this special market turn to for advice? What turns them on? What turns them off?

_____

_____

10. How can you communicate with this special market? What do you say to them? How do you say it? Where do you say it? When do you say it?

_____

_____

75

Working with Numbers
& Tables: 14 Tips

A table must display numbers in a way that will be clearly and easily understood, that will catch the eye, and that will intrigue the mind. Many people have trouble understanding numbers. Here are 14 tips for working with numbers and using them in tables.

1. Show no more detail than is needed. Instead of saying, "SuperWhiz spent $13,683,976," say "SuperWhiz spent $13.7 million."

2. Never put too much information in one table. The mind simply won't grasp it, and its usefulness will be destroyed.

3. Show the source of your data beneath a table so that anyone wanting more information knows where to get it.

4. When using a bar graph, arrange the bars from high to low or low to high. It will be much easier for readers to remember the information than if the bars are in alphabetical order.

5. Use bar graphs to show relationships among numbers, and line graphs to show trends over time.

6. Do you want a table to read from left to right or top to bottom? Use the layout that reads the easiest and makes your point the quickest. It will vary from table to table.

7. Column headings help to reduce the numbers in a table. This bad example includes 21 numbers while the good example has only seven:

	Bad	Good
	Dollars	$(million)
Advertising	$12,580,000	$12.6
Direct Marketing	3,940,000	3.9
Events	480,000	0.5

8. Suppose a table is headed "%." If one number in the table is supposed to be 4%, use "4." If you put the decimal equivalent of 0.04 under a "%" heading in a table, you are really showing only $4/100$ of 1%.

9. Let the title of a table highlight a key point. Instead of this:

Annual Sales by Region

Region	1993 Sales $(MM)	1994 Sales $(MM)	% Change
East	1,234	1,342	+ 9
Midwest	934	1,308	+ 40
West	1,023	1,123	+ 10
South	1,123	1,239	+ 10

Say this:

Midwest Sales Jump 40% in 1994

Region	1993 Sales $(MM)	1994 Sales $(MM)	% Change
East	1,234	1,342	+ 9
Midwest	934	1,308	+ 40
West	1,023	1,123	+ 10
South	1,123	1,239	+ 10

10. Numbers in a report come alive and are easier to remember if you vary how you describe them. For example, you can refer to 78% in many ways:

- 78% of the homes own a VCR.
- More than three out of four homes own a VCR.
- Nearly 8 out of 10 homes own a VCR.
- Nearly four out of five homes own a VCR.
- More than 3/4 of the homes own a VCR.

11. The detail you show depends on the end use of the data. If you are going to order 20 million pairs of 3-D glasses, and your CEO asks how much they will cost, it's fine to say "about $1 million, or close to 5 cents each." If, however, you want him to see the competitive bids, you need more detail. In the following example, each $0.001 equals $20,000!

	Cost Per Pair	Total Cost
ABC Co.	.0475	$ 950,000
MNO Co.	.0495	990,000
XYZ Co.	.0515	1,030,000

12. All numbers in a column *must* be carried to the same decimal level.

	Not OK	OK	or	OK
XX	32	32		32.0
YY	29.2	29		29.2
ZZ	6.78	7		6.8

13. Readers of a table are frustrated if the numbers in a column do not all add up to the total shown. If there is a good reason why they don't (something is included in each of two areas) explain it beneath the table.

14. Do you want a number to stand out? Make it stand out!

Acme Leads In All Popcorn Category Sales

	Share of Sales (%)		
	Plain	Cheese	Chocolate
Acme	47	65	50
Tops	33	15	25
Zesty	20	20	25
Total	100	100	100

Part VIII

Communicating to Win

"It's not just what you know...it's how you show you know it!"

It's simple, but true: in marketing communications, communication is critical. To succeed, you must write well, present well, negotiate well, *and* build lasting relationships with your clients and customers. The fifteen checklists and charts in Part VIII will help you polish all aspects of your communications skills.

76. 14 Tips to a Winning Presentation
77. 6 Steps to Learning from Failure
78. 10 Guidelines to Communicating across Cultures
79. Guidelines for Using Numbers in Presentations
80. The "Never-to-Be-Forgotten" Pocket Presentation Planner
81. Negotiating to Win: 9 Tips
82. Winning at New Business: 11 Guidelines
83. 30 Ways for an Agency to Establish Good Client Relations
84. When Should You Put It in Writing?
85. More Effective Business Writing: A 3-Step Approach
86. Writing for Information: A 7-Step Approach
87. Writing an Effective Sales Letter: A 4-Step Checklist
88. 7 Tips for More Productive Meetings
89. Conferences and Special Events: A 151-Item Checklist
90. 6 Tips for Efficient Filing

76

14 Tips to a Winning Presentation

Whether you are speaking before hundreds in a hotel ballroom or a single client in a conference room, the success of your presentation depends on more than what you have to say. How you say it and how you interact with your audience also determine their response. These 14 guidelines are aimed at making you and your presentation winners with your audience.

1. Be sure to tell your audience why your presentation is relevant to them.

2. Keep your presentation within or under the amount of time you have been allowed. Research indicates that adult concentration peaks out at 1 hour and 15 minutes. If you plan to allow 30 minutes for questions and discussion, spend no more than 45 minutes on your formal presentation.

3. Do not tell jokes unless you are a great storyteller...and then make certain that your story will offend absolutely no one in the room!

4. Remember that most audiences do not settle down right away. Don't make clever statements and important points in the first minutes of your presentation.

5. Eliminate all material that is not directly relevant to the central theme of your presentation.

6. Your visual aids should be aids and not crutches. Do not overwhelm your audience with them.

7. Make certain the visual aids are large enough for everyone in the audience to see and simple enough for everyone to understand.

8. Visuals should relate only to that portion of the presentation you are covering at a particular point in time. Never permit your audience to look ahead on the screen to something you are not yet ready to discuss.

9. Maintain eye contact with your audience throughout your presentation.

14 Tips to a Winning Presentation

10. Make sure your podium microphone and light are in good working order.

11. During the question period, you are bound to hear from people who aren't really asking questions, but are giving a speech designed to show how much they know or how much more they know than you do. Respect them, but never be defensive. Emphasize the points upon which you agree, and point out those that you do not agree with.

12. Listen actively to audience questions. Often, the questioner is asking more than what meets the ear.

13. Always rephrase what you think the question to be before you respond to it.

14. Expect to have pictures taken at many events where you will speak. Dress professionally and in colors that photograph well. This means dark colors rather than light tones, contrasting shirts and blouses, and bright ties or scarves.

6 Steps to Learning from Failure

From childhood, we are all told that we should learn from our mistakes.

But do we?

Or do we continue to make the same mistakes over and over again?

Memorize these six questions; or better still, carry them around with you on a small 3 × 5 card. Adhere to them, and it's guaranteed they will save you time, money, and much stress.

1. What really went wrong?

_____

_____

2. Do I really understand how, when, where, and why it went wrong?

_____

_____

3. What should I have done?

_____

_____

4. What shouldn't I have done?

_____

_____

5. What will I do to ensure that I don't make the same mistakes again?

_____

_____

6. If I can't correct these mistakes myself, to whom can I turn for help?

_____

_____

10 Guidelines for Communicating across Cultures

In today's global marketing economy, there are still many significant differences among countries in terms of language, lifestyle, culture, likes and dislikes, business procedures, ways of thinking, etc. The most effective presentation in one country can be totally misunderstood in another if it does not take these differences into account. When giving a presentation outside of the United States, always follow these ten guidelines.

1. Even if everyone in the room speaks English, they will probably not understand many terms we take for granted. Avoid using them.

2. If you want to speak the language used in another country, make sure you can do it well—or stick with your own language.

3. Study the many local customs and policies of the country to avoid offending anyone in the room.

4. Start simply, speak slowly, and warm up your audience. Never dive right into the most important parts of your presentation.

5. If you use charts, slides, or overheads, make certain that what they say is the same as what you are saying. Otherwise, your audience will be totally confused.

6. It is hard enough to tell a good joke in front of an audience in this country. Outside of the United States, it's better to skip them.

7. If you feel that using a translator will be helpful, do so. But make sure the translator is a professional and insist on simultaneous translation.

8. To make certain that your audience understands what you are saying, take frequent "question breaks."

9. Many people outside of the United States are shy. They will hesitate to ask about something they do not understand. If you are uncertain as to whether they understand what you are saying, assume they do not.

10. A speaker at a large conference here may arrive only a few minutes before his or her presentation. Outside of the United States, be a part of the audience well in advance of your presentation. Get to know your audience. Observe how they respond to others on the program.

Guidelines for Using Numbers in Presentations

In more than one presentation, you've probably seen a number and wondered where it came from, what it meant, and what you were expected to do with it. Follow these guidelines and you will have won the battle of figure frustration!

1. Make certain to indicate where numbers came from.

2. When you are showing a trend, define its base period exactly.

3. When you show percentages or index numbers, be sure to include the real numbers themselves to avoid any misleading assumptions.

4. Be sure to show long-term trends and not just averages at one or two points in time.

5. Use the most up-to-date numbers you have, but if they are not typical of a long-term trend, be sure to indicate so.

6. Because most people have trouble with numbers, use tables, charts, and graphs whenever possible.

7. When you use tables, use several of them rather than crowding everything into one.

8. Bring the numbers alive, and clearly explain to everyone what they mean.

The "Never-to-Be-Forgotten" Pocket Presentation Planner

As the name implies, this should be carried into every meeting where an upcoming presentation may be discussed. Its purpose is to make certain that when you leave the meeting, you can pass on to your associates just what the presentation will cover and what is expected of whom.

THE OCCASION

Purpose of the Presentation?

_____

_____

_____

When?

_____

_____

_____

Where?

_____

_____

_____

How Long?

_____

_____

_____

The Pocket Presentation Planner

THE AUDIENCE

Who?

_____

_____

_____

How Many?

_____

_____

_____

Knowledge of Subject?

_____

_____

_____

Background?

_____

_____

_____

Going-In Opinions?

_____

_____

_____

The Pocket Presentation Planner

WHAT TO INCLUDE

Information?   Provided by Whom?   Ways to Visualize?

_____   _____   _____

_____   _____   _____

_____   _____   _____

_____   _____   _____

_____   _____   _____

_____   _____   _____

_____   _____   _____

_____   _____   _____

_____   _____   _____

_____   _____   _____

_____   _____   _____

_____   _____   _____

_____   _____   _____

_____   _____   _____

_____   _____   _____

_____   _____   _____

_____   _____   _____

_____   _____   _____

_____   _____   _____

_____   _____   _____

81

Negotiating to Win: 9 Tips

In a negotiation, there is one basic objective . . . to win. And the key to winning is having a leg up in terms of knowledge and technique. While volumes have been written on how to negotiate, success in the end really depends on these two points. By carefully considering each of the following questions, you'll get that leg up and prepare yourself for even the toughest negotiation.

	YES	NO
1. Are you absolutely sure you are negotiating with the right person—the person with the power?	☐	☐
2. Do you have any insights into the people you are negotiating with that can help you win?	☐	☐
3. Do you know what you really want to accomplish?	☐	☐
4. Do you know what you are really willing to give in on to accomplish this?	☐	☐
5. Have you done all of your homework and gathered all of the facts you need to support your position?	☐	☐

	YES	NO

6. Are you negotiating on neutral turf? ☐ ☐

_____

_____

7. Is time on your side or are you being pressured to make a fast decision? ☐ ☐

_____

_____

8. Will you be able to convince the other side that if you win, they won't lose—or better still, that if you win, they win? ☐ ☐

_____

_____

9. Are you certain that now is the best time to be entering into the negotiation? ☐ ☐

_____

_____

82

Winning at New Business: 11 Guidelines

An advertising agency's growth depends on how well it keeps its existing clients satisfied and how successfully it wins new business. Often, the difference between winning and losing a new business presentation is small— so small that the losing agency may say, "If only I had . . . ." *Winning at New Business: 11 Guidelines* will improve your odds.

1. Focus exclusively on the client, his or her concerns and interests throughout the presentation. The client doesn't really care how wonderful you are. What the client does care about is what's in it for him or her.

   Notes: _____

   _____

   _____

2. Every good salesperson knows that if you don't get your customer's attention right at the start, you may have lost him or her forever. Each minute counts so don't waste a precious second by being boring or irrelevant.

   Notes: _____

   _____

   _____

3. Never let your audiovisuals dominate the presentation. In the end, it is the person-to-person chemistry that is critical.

   Notes: _____

   _____

   _____

4. Don't overdo the case histories. If a case study cannot be related to the client's business and how you can help make it grow, don't use up time presenting it.

   Notes: _____

   _____

   _____

Guidelines for Winning at New Business

5. Avoid showing too much of your work. Every agency you compete with can be expected to show its very best work—so thin out anything that isn't your very, very best.

Notes: _____

_____

_____

6. Don't line up too many presenters. It is difficult to tell someone who has worked hard pulling a presentation together that he or she won't be in the meeting itself. But clients do not like to feel overwhelmed. Limit your team to a small number of professionals who are first-rate presenters and who will play a significant role in the meeting.

Notes: _____

_____

_____

7. If the meeting is on your turf, make sure the physical surroundings are comfortable. If the first thing a prospective client says is, "It's too hot in here," you face an uphill battle.

Notes: _____

_____

_____

8. Every agency will promise A+ work. Just as one brand must differentiate itself from others in its category, your agency must offer a unique focus that separates it from the competition.

Notes: _____

_____

_____

9. Sell the steak, but don't forget that the sizzle may get you the business. Given the choice between a dull, dependable shop and an exciting, slightly risky agency, excitement will usually win out.

Notes: _____

_____

_____

10. At one time, large, full-service agencies regarded other large, full-service agencies as their only competition. No longer. Today, advertisers can provide many of the services offered by the larger agencies in-house or through independent media services and consultants. Don't overdue bigness!

Notes: _____

_____

_____

11. And finally, never *ever* forget to let your prospective client know that you really want the client's business. And never forget to ask for the order!

Notes: _____

_____

_____

30 Ways for an Agency to Establish Good Client Relations

Mergers, acquisitions, increasing profit pressure, and advertiser unrest have made the need for strong agency-client relations greater than ever. During her many years in account management at DDB Needham Worldwide, Robbie Boudreau compiled this list of *30 Ways for an Agency to Establish Good Client Relations.* Use it to check up on the state of your agency-client marriage. Note the rocky areas, and focus on how you can build a stronger relationship in the future. Much of this is just pure common sense. But unfortunately, common sense is what we too often overlook in our relations with one another!

Should I Work on This?

	YES	NO
1. Be dependable.	☐	☐
2. Be knowledgeable about your agency's resources.	☐	☐
3. Be knowledgeable about your client's business.	☐	☐
4. Cultivate a team spirit between you and your immediate counterpart at the client.	☐	☐
5. Be honest. Never lie to your client.	☐	☐
6. Be proactive and show initiative. Don't just take orders from your client.	☐	☐
7. Be a problem solver, not a problem maker!	☐	☐
8. Be perceptive. Know your client's likes, dislikes, and idiosyncrasies.	☐	☐
9. Champion the development of outstanding work for your client by your agency.	☐	☐
10. Be friends with your client.	☐	☐
11. Go that extra mile beyond simply fulfilling your client's requests.	☐	☐
12. Make your client look good in front of his boss and his management.	☐	☐
13. Know your client's birthday, anniversary, and favorite restaurants.	☐	☐
14. Be human and be yourself, so that the client does not see you as a clone of the agency.	☐	☐

Ways to Establish Good Client Relations

	YES	NO
15. Keep your client up-to-date and knowledgeable about what's happening in advertising. Send him or her articles, commercials, examples of great and bad advertising.	☐	☐
16. Make sure your client believes you are truly an advertising expert.	☐	☐
17. Do the little things that make a difference, like bringing in the donuts for an early morning meeting.	☐	☐
18. Don't constantly badger your client about the need to spend more in media. Be ready to make the point when the time is right, but don't beat it into the ground.	☐	☐
19. Develop a good relationship with your client's secretary.	☐	☐
20. Return your client's phone calls within a reasonable period of time.	☐	☐
21. Know the names of all your client's children.	☐	☐
22. Explain why something can't be done in a certain way by a certain time—but don't make excuses.	☐	☐
23. Never copy your client's supervisor without telling him or her you are doing so.	☐	☐
24. Don't use old advertising cliches like "impactful," "proactive," and "we're really excited about this breakthrough creative."	☐	☐
25. Don't promise that which you know cannot be delivered.	☐	☐
26. Don't cry wolf by always getting excited about everything. Save your steam for the things that really count.	☐	☐
27. Help your client develop close relationships with all the key people at the agency who work on his or her business.	☐	☐
28. Don't be so intent on winning every battle with your client that you eventually lose the war.	☐	☐
29. Be prudent with your client's money. Recommend ways to improve the efficiency of media buys and production budgets. Find ways to save your client money.	☐	☐
30. Be enthusiastic!	☐	☐

When Should You Put It in Writing?

In today's business climate, there is a constant conflict between the desire to keep it simple and the tendency to overdo it. This affects the communications process when you must decide between putting a message in writing or conveying it in person or over the phone. Because time is money, your decision should depend upon your answers to the following eight questions. If you answer "Yes" to any one of them, write it out!

	YES	NO
1. Are you concerned that what you have to say will not be understood or properly acted upon?	☐	☐
2. If the message is misunderstood, will it cost you time and/or money?	☐	☐
3. Are you asking people to spend their own time and/or money on something?	☐	☐
4. Are you attempting to change a way of doing something that has been long understood and accepted?	☐	☐
5. Do a large number of people need to receive, understand, and act upon the same message?	☐	☐
6. Will you and the people who follow you need to know what was said in the days, weeks, months, and years ahead?	☐	☐
7. Is what you have to say more than just a routine request or question?	☐	☐
8. Will you sleep better knowing that it is in writing?	☐	☐

More Effective Business Writing: A 3-Step Approach

Whether you write business reports, memos, and letters every day or just once in a while, this three-step approach can make writing easier and make what you write more effective. Just remember, *follow all three steps.* Prewriting is as essential as the actual writing itself—and without revising, the most important document may be hopelessly unprofessional.

Step One: Prewriting

In prewriting, you are defining your concept and gathering facts that will serve as material for step two, writing. Ask yourself these questions first.

1. What is the purpose of what you are writing? Why are you writing it?

2. Who is the audience you want to inform or influence? What are their interests and motivations? How much knowledge and interest will they have in what you say?

3. What do you want to say, and what is the scope of the project?

4. How much and what kind of background research data do you need to gather?

Step Two: Writing

After you have established your purpose, identified your audience, defined your topic, and gathered your data, you are ready to write.

1. Determine how you can most effectively organize the material to clearly and completely communicate what you have to say.

2. Outline what you want to say in the order you want to say it.

3. Write the first draft, concentrating on developing what you want to say and not concentrating on the exact form in which you say it.

Step Three: Revising

When you begin to revise your material, keep in mind that you are reading it primarily from the *reader's* point of view.

1. Edit and check the draft several times for clarity, tone, accuracy, and brevity. Have you included everything your reader will want to know to make a decision?

2. Check for grammar, spelling errors, and other careless mistakes.

3. Make sure the final copy is neat and free from erasures, typos, and other marks.

Source: *Handbook for Business Writing,* by L. Sue Baugh, Maridell Fryar, and David Thomas (1994).

Writing for Information: A 7-Step Approach

When you write for information, you want the person receiving your letter to understand what you need and send the material out to you promptly. Follow these seven steps to avoid needless confusion and back-and-forth communication.

1. Clearly state exactly what type of information you are requesting.

2. Ask only for that information you believe the respondent will be able to supply.

3. Explain why you need the information and why it is important for the person you are writing to supply it.

4. Express your appreciation for the time they have taken to read and consider your request.

5. Let your reader know a realistic date by which you need to receive the information.

6. Indicate your willingness to cover the cost of any materials the reader may send you.

7. When you feel it is appropriate, include a self-addressed, stamped envelope. It is thoughtful, helpful, and can often speed up the delivery of the information to you.

Source: *Handbook for Business Writing,* by L. Sue Baugh, Maridell Fryar, and David Thomas (1994).

Writing an Effective Sales Letter: A 4-Step Checklist

The growing focus on direct marketing has resulted in a dramatic increase in the number of sales letters delivered to mailboxes across the country every day of the week. An effective sales letter represents money in the cash register, and *Writing an Effective Sales Letter: A 4-Step Checklist* can help ring the register for you.

Step One: Grab the Reader's Attention

                                                            YES   NO

1. Have you identified the reader's needs and interests?   ☐   ☐

   Suggested Improvement: _____

   _____

   _____

2. What benefits does your product or service offer the reader?   ☐   ☐

   Suggested Improvement: _____

   _____

   _____

3. Can you state the benefit in a question or arresting statement?   ☐   ☐

   Suggested Improvement: _____

   _____

   _____

Step Two: Interest the Reader in What You Have to Say

1. What motivations are you addressing—profit, savings, comfort, convenience, prestige, or something else?   ☐   ☐

   Suggested Improvement: _____

   _____

   _____

Checklist for Writing an Effective Sales Letter

2. If the reader has a problem you have identified, does your product or service offer a solution? ☐   ☐

   Suggested Improvement: _____

   _____

   _____

3. Did you point out what emotional satisfaction the reader would gain from your product or service? ☐   ☐

   Suggested Improvement: _____

   _____

   _____

Step Three: Create Desire for What You Are Selling

1. Have you supported your statements with interesting facts, statistics, tests, and/or testimonials? ☐   ☐

   Suggested Improvement: _____

   _____

   _____

2. Did you offer any warranty, money-back promise, or evidence of your support for your product or service? ☐   ☐

   Suggested Improvement: _____

   _____

   _____

Checklist for Writing an Effective Sales Letter

Step Four: Ask the Reader to Take Action Now!	YES	NO

1. What specific action do you want the reader to take? ☐ ☐

   Suggested Improvement: _____

   _____

   _____

2. Did you avoid alternative or ambiguous choices? ☐ ☐

   Suggested Improvement: _____

   _____

   _____

3. Have you made it easy for the reader to act? ☐ ☐

   Suggested Improvement: _____

   _____

   _____

4. Is your desired action the last sentence in the letter? ☐ ☐

   Suggested Improvement: _____

   _____

   _____

Source: *Handbook for Business Writing,* by L. Sue Baugh, Maridell Fryar, and David Thomas (1994).

7 Tips for More Productive Meetings

Marketing communicators constantly complain about the meetings they attend—how most of them are boring, unnecessary, and too time consuming. The secret to a good meeting is having a plan and sticking to it. That's what these *7 Tips for More Productive Meetings* are all about.

1. Before calling a meeting, ask yourself, "Is this meeting really necessary?"

2. If it is, then be sure to have a written agenda. Distribute it in advance so everyone knows what will be covered.

3. Invite only those people to the meeting who need to be there.

4. If you have lots of material to cover, take care of the easiest, most positive items first.

5. Since you have an agenda, stick to it!

6. Never end a meeting without evaluating it. What was good? What was bad? What will you change at the next meeting?

7. Finally, always remember that if you call a meeting, it is your meeting to lead. Run it. Don't let it run you.

Conferences and Special Events: A 151-Item Checklist

"For want of a nail, the shoe was lost. For want of a shoe, the horse was lost. For want of a horse, the message was lost. For want of a message, the battle was lost." Anyone who has ever organized or planned a meeting would agree, "For want of a projection bulb, coffee, or a nonsmoking section, the meeting was lost!" Robert Roth's Checklist covers 151 "forget-me-nots" essential to the success of any major gathering.

Starting Checklist

☐ 1. Recruit help

☐ 2. Appoint committee chairpersons for:
☐   Site selection
☐   Agenda
☐   Delegates
☐   Finance
☐   Transportation
☐   Registration

☐   Banquet
☐   Entertainment
☐   After-hours activities

☐ 3. Firm up choice of hotel

☐ 4. Arrange for monthly progress reports

☐ 5. Final report three months before meeting/seminar/convention

Accommodations Checklist

☐ 1. Total of rooms needed:
☐   Singles
☐   Doubles
☐   Suites

☐ 2. Room rates

☐ 3. Roll-away beds for children

☐ 4. Reservations to be confirmed by hotel

☐ 5. Date majority arriving

☐ 6. Check-in time limits

☐ 7. Date majority departing

☐ 8. Check-out time

☐ 9. Special VIP arrangements

☐ 10. Hospitality areas

☐ 11. Nonalcoholic hospitality suites

☐ 12. Parking garage facilities

☐ 13. Food plan
☐   AP (American Plan)
☐   MAP (Modified American Plan)
☐   European Plan

☐ 14. Credit arrangements agreed for guests

Registration Checklist

☐ 1. Procedure for guests

☐ 2. Procedure for VIPs

☐ 3. Welcoming service

☐ 4. Signs for registration desk

☐ 5. Lobby registration table if required

☐ 6. Identification badges

☐ 7. Wastebaskets

☐ 8. Hospitality rooms

☐ 9. Emergency spare rooms

☐ 10. Facilities guide

☐ 11. Agenda displayed

☐ 12. Consult hotel credit manager

☐ 13. Experts to handle money

☐ 14. Literature distributed

☐ 15. Checklists to committee members

Checklist for Conferences and Special Events

Speakers Checklist

☐ 1. Arrangements made well before meeting
☐ 2. Time speaker to be available
☐ 3. Place speaker to be available
☐ 4. Length of talk
☐ 5. Type of talk planned
☐ 6. Fee fixed
☐ 7. Expenses arranged including transportation
☐ 8. Biographical notes for introduction
☐ 9. Photograph for literature and publicity
☐ 10. Hospitality for spouse
☐ 11. Hotel reservation(s) made
☐ 12. Special equipment provided
☐ 13. Program supplied to speaker
☐ 14. Special guest(s) to be invited
☐ 15. Speaker to be met at airport/station
☐ 16. Introduced to officers, VIPs
☐ 17. Alternative speaker available
☐ 18. Flowers, refreshments, fruit in room

Bird Dog Checklist

☐ 1. Set up agenda
☐ 2. Set up daily routines
☐ 3. Arrangements made with hotel
☐ 4. All telephone numbers noted
☐ 5. All times noted
☐ 6. Literature for distribution
☐ 7. Welcoming arrangements made
☐ 8. Get-acquainted party
☐ 9. Formal welcoming speech

Meeting Rooms Checklist

☐ 1. Sufficient seats
☐ 2. . . .properly arranged
☐ 3. Place cards correct
☐ 4. Pads, pencils distributed
☐ 5. . . .and ash trays; glasses, water pitchers
☐ 6. Nonsmoking section
☐ 7. Light switches located and in working order
☐ 8. Cooling, heating controls located and checked
☐ 9. Stage equipment checked
☐ 10. Lectern ready, light working, gavel in place
☐ 11. All arrangements made for speakers
☐ 12. Speaker's pointer handy
☐ 13. Microphone checked
☐ 14. Loudspeaker in place
☐ 15. Volume adjusted
☐ 16. Extension cord no hazard
☐ 17. Easel, markers ready
☐ 18. Projection screen installed
☐ 19. Projection equipment plugged in
☐ 20. Projection lamp tested
☐ 21. Screen correct size
☐ 22. Screen correctly positioned
☐ 23. Audience view unobstructed
☐ 24. Spare lamps and fuses ready
☐ 25. Lenses clean
☐ 26. Directional signs posted
☐ 27. Rest rooms indicated
☐ 28. Member of your staff at door if necessary
☐ 29. Room(s) booked for guest speaker(s)

Checklist for Conferences and Special Events

Visual Aids Checklist

Choose among:

- ☐ 1. Easel pad and felt markers
- ☐ 2. Overhead projector
- ☐ 3. Slide presentation
- ☐ 4. Movie and video equipment
- ☐ 5. Closed-circuit television

Also:

- ☐ 6. Check projection screen size

Coffee/Cocktails Checklist

- ☐ 1. Place to serve coffee
- ☐ 2. Check coffee arrangement
- ☐ 3. Supply decaffeinated coffee
- ☐ 4. Sugar substitutes
- ☐ 5. Tea
- ☐ 6. Soft drinks
- ☐ 7. Arrangements to close bar
- ☐ 8. Appoint one person only who can keep bar open

Banquet Checklist

- ☐ 1. Seating arrangements
- ☐ 2. Speeches kept short by agreement
- ☐ 3. Plan menu with banquet sales manager
- ☐ 4. Wines—to serve or not to serve
- ☐ 5. Champagne—yes or no
- ☐ 6. Spectacular dishes—yes or no

Day-to-Day Meals Checklist

- ☐ 1. Check menus
- ☐ 2. Consult hotel's food and beverage manager
- ☐ 3. . . .or banquet manager
- ☐ 4. . . .or maitre d'hotel
- ☐ 5. Breakfast—buffet-style
- ☐ 6. Lunch—light, especially dessert
- ☐ 7. All meals—varied with alternative choices

Entertainment Checklist

- ☐ 1. Check budget. . .
- ☐ 2. . . .allow for emergencies
- ☐ 3. Professional entertainers only
- ☐ 4. Seek local talent
- ☐ 5. Show to suit audience
- ☐ 6. Family routine or nightclub
- ☐ 7. Dressing room(s) for artist(s)
- ☐ 8. Union regulations followed
- ☐ 9. Arrangements for payment
- ☐ 10. Arrangements for standby
- ☐ 11. Arrangements for artist payments

Checklist for Conferences and Special Events

After-Hours Relaxation Checklist

☐ 1. Keep activities affordable

☐ 2. Stagger meeting hours for fun

☐ 3. Plan a pre- or post-meeting tour

Spouses Checklist

☐ 1. Plan program thoroughly

☐ 2. Know general interest

☐ 3. Consider budget

☐ 4. Consider spouses' budgets

☐ 5. Spouses' hospitality suite—staffing

☐ 6. Schedule function outside hotel for variety

☐ 7. Check for group-rate savings on activities

☐ 8. Arrange guide for bus trip

☐ 9. Arrange cultural tours

☐ 10. Fashion show

☐ 11. Arrange suitable speaker for spouses-only lecture

Printed Literature Checklist

☐ 1. Pocket program

☐ 2. Program

☐ 3. List of participants

☐ 4. Menu

☐ 5. Texts of speeches

☐ 6. Texts of panel discussions

☐ 7. Spouses' program

☐ 8. Seating plan

☐ 9. Tour program

Source: *International Marketing Communications*, by Robert F. Roth (1982).

6 Tips for Efficient Filing

The most common complaints about filing systems are "I am saving too many things" and "I can't find anything I have saved!" These *6 Tips for Efficient Filing* should help alleviate both problems.

1. What information do you absolutely need to have right in your office at your fingertips?

_____

_____

2. What material can you keep in files outside your office?

_____

_____

3. What material is being kept (or should be kept) by other people?

_____

_____

4. What material should be thrown out?

_____

_____

5. Have you kept a list of your major file labels so you know what you have and where it is?

_____

_____

6. Is there a system to your filing that others can figure out?

_____

_____

Part IX

The Job, Money, and Travel Survival Kit

The life of every marketer is far more hectic today than it was a decade ago. This book would, therefore, never be complete without a *personal* survival kit. That's what Part IX is all about. It focuses exclusively on Y-O-U. Its eight checklists and charts are aimed at getting a job, traveling on business, and saving on income tax.

91. The Job Hunting Action Planner

92. The Resume Planning Form

93. 11 Questions to Ask Yourself about a Prospective Employee

94. The Marketing Communicator's Income Tax Saver

95. The Not-to-Be-Forgotten Business Traveler's Checklist

96. Fitness on the Move

97. The Business Traveler's Basic Health Kit

98. 12 Tips to Keep Long-Distance Travel from Becoming Travail

The Job Hunting
Action Planner

Mergers and acquisitions, consolidations, and a fluctuating economy have dramatically affected employment opportunities in the marketing communications industry. Executive recruiters emphasize the importance of following an organized and systematic approach in the job hunt process. *The Job Hunting Action Planner* will keep your job search on track while you plan your next step. Individual sheets should be kept for each company, and the appropriate spaces should be filled out after each meeting or phone conversation.

Company _____

Address _____

Name and Title _____

_____

Department _____

Phone _____

Secretary _____

Action _____

_____

Date _____

Results _____

_____

Next Step _____

_____

Comments _____

_____

The Resume Planning Form

A resume, your "Personal Presentation in Print," should give the most complete picture possible of who you are and what you can contribute to a company. It should be concise, easy to follow, attractive, and act as an enticement to your prospective employer to want to find out more about you. Experience has shown that the following one-page format works very well.

Name _____

Address _____

_____

Telephone _____ (Day)

_____ (Night)

Job Objective

_____

Experience

Job Title _____ Dates _____

Employer _____

Duties & Accomplishments _____

_____

_____

Experience

Job Title _____ Dates _____

Employer _____

Duties & Accomplishments _____

_____

_____

The Resume Planning Form

Experience

Job Title _____ Dates _____

Employer _____

Duties & Accomplishments _____

_____

_____

Education (Number as relevant)

Degree _____ Dates _____

School _____

Major _____

Minor _____

Education (Number as relevant)

Degree _____ Dates _____

School _____

Major _____

Minor _____

Special Skills and Interests

_____

Honors, Awards, Publications, Presentations

_____

Relevant Personal Information

_____

References (Optional)

_____

93

11 Questions to Ask Yourself about a Prospective Employee

Interviewing a prospective job candidate can be a very tough assignment. A company is often so anxious to fill a slot that it leaps to hire without looking hard enough at the kind of job a prospect can be expected to do. Ask yourself each of the following questions before making that crucial final hiring decision. If you answer "No" to any question, rethink your decision and get a second opinion. And remember: if *you* are interviewing for a job, your prospective employer will want to know *your* answers to these same questions!

	YES	NO
1. When I put together everything I know about this person, do I really believe he or she can do the job?	☐	☐

Why? _____

_____

| 2. Will this person quickly learn how to handle new responsibilities and respond to change? | ☐ | ☐ |

Why? _____

_____

| 3. Does this person really want this job more than any other position? | ☐ | ☐ |

Why? _____

_____

| 4. Does he or she want to work for our company or is it merely a stepping-stone to another company? | ☐ | ☐ |

Why? _____

_____

| 5. Does the candidate have the education, training, and experience for the job? | ☐ | ☐ |

Why? _____

_____

Questions to Ask about a Prospective Employee

	YES	NO

6. Does he or she have the specific skills and knowledge needed to carry out the job effectively and efficiently?   ☐   ☐

   Why? _____

   _____

7. Does the candidate lead a balanced life with interests that extend beyond work?   ☐   ☐

   Why? _____

   _____

8. Will he or she get along with superiors, fellow workers, subordinates, and clients?   ☐   ☐

   Why? _____

   _____

9. Will the candidate think for himself or herself, act on what he or she thinks, and know when to consult with the boss?   ☐   ☐

   Why? _____

   _____

10. Will this person be sensitive to the traditions of the company and to its ways of doing things?   ☐   ☐

    Why? _____

    _____

11. Will the job candidate's skills and knowledge fit in with those of other employees, and will he or she fill in the gaps that need filling?   ☐   ☐

    Why? _____

    _____

Source: *How to Have a Winning Job Interview*, by Deborah Perlmutter Bloch (1992).

94

The Marketing Communicator's Income Tax Saver

It's not what you make, it's what you keep! And there are a whole host of deductible items every marketing communicator should be aware of. Just remember that they must be itemized and related to your business, and that they are subject to limitations imposed by the IRS.

	This Applies to Me	
	YES	NO
VCR	☐	☐
Television set, cable television costs	☐	☐
Camera (regular and video)	☐	☐
Personal computer	☐	☐
Audio tape recorder	☐	☐
Stereo	☐	☐
Tapes	☐	☐
Video rentals and membership dues	☐	☐
Cellular phone	☐	☐
Your portfolio and reels	☐	☐
Foul weather gear for filming commercials on location	☐	☐
Theater, movie, and sporting event tickets used as a part of client research	☐	☐
Membership dues	☐	☐
Award show entry fees	☐	☐
Books, professional magazines, and newspapers	☐	☐
Home office furniture, desk, cabinets	☐	☐
Office pictures	☐	☐
Frames for award certificates	☐	☐
Club and credit card dues	☐	☐
Home telephone calls	☐	☐
Telephone answering machine, voice-mail, etc.	☐	☐

The Marketing Communicator's Income Tax Saver

	This Applies to Me	
	YES	**NO**
Home entertaining	☐	☐
Tux rental and the cost of cleaning formal wear	☐	☐
Parking at office to have car available for client business	☐	☐
All free-lance and research expenses, including travel, resumes, and out-of-town meals	☐	☐
Business gifts and gifts to secretary	☐	☐
Nonreimbursed business expenses	☐	☐

Other items I want to ask my accountant about:

	YES	NO
_____	☐	☐
_____	☐	☐
_____	☐	☐
_____	☐	☐
_____	☐	☐
_____	☐	☐
_____	☐	☐
_____	☐	☐
_____	☐	☐
_____	☐	☐
_____	☐	☐
_____	☐	☐
_____	☐	☐
_____	☐	☐

Source: *Pay Less Tax Legally,* by Barry R. Steiner, CPA.

95

The Not-to-Be-Forgotten
Business Traveler's Checklist

If you've never had to buy a tube of toothpaste, a shirt, or a pair of sunglasses on a business trip, you're in the minority. And if you have, you know how aggravating it is. It takes time, and you pay twice as much at your hotel as you would at home. The solution to the problem? *The Not-to-Be-Forgotten Business Traveler's Checklist.* It's guaranteed to save you time, money, and frustration.

Men's Clothing	Women's Clothing	Toiletries & Accessories
Suits	Suits	Toothbrush/toothpaste
Sport jackets	Skirts	Deodorant
Slacks	Dresses	Shampoo/conditioner
Shirts	Slacks	Razor and blades
Sweaters	Blouses	Shaving cream
Shoes	Sweaters	Hair dryer
Socks	Shoes	Makeup
Slippers	Stockings	Personal products
Pajamas	Slippers	Comb and brush
Robe	Nightgown	Extra glasses/sunglasses
Underwear	Robe	Tanning lotion/sunscreen
Ties	Underclothing	Camera and film
Belts	Scarves and ties	Travel tickets
Sportswear	Belts	Passport
Handkerchiefs	Sportswear	Alarm clock
Jacket	Handkerchiefs	Exercise equipment
Hat	Jacket	Umbrella
Raincoat	Hat	Laptop computer
Boots or rubbers	Raincoat	Cellular phone
Formal wear	Boots or rubbers	Work to be done

_____ _____ _____

_____ _____ _____

_____ _____ _____

_____ _____ _____

_____ _____ _____

_____ _____ _____

_____ _____ _____

Fitness on the Move

Out-of-town trips may cut into your normal exercise routine, but business travel need not result in fitness travail. A brisk, 15- to 20-minute walk can help your heart, your lungs, your blood pressure, *and* your waistline. It can make you feel better, think better, and perform better. Just keep the following points in mind.

1. Dress comfortably and wear sturdy running or walking shoes.

2. Stretch and bend for a few minutes to warm up before your walk.

3. Walk with your toes pointed straight ahead, head up, back straight, arms loosely swinging at your side.

4. Take long, easy strides. You're not out to break any time or distance records.

5. Breathe steadily and deeply. If you feel out of breath, *slow down*.

6. Walk before eating. Never exercise immediately after a meal.

7. Relax and have fun. Don't make your walk work!

The Business Traveler's
Basic Health Kit

Marketing communicators do a lot of traveling. And one of life's great frustrations is finding yourself in a strange city in need of medication. You will probably remember to take along the obvious. But before you leave home, contact your doctor or pharmacist for specific recommendations as to what you should take with you to prevent or control less familiar problems.

	Needed?	Recommended Medication
Headaches		
Earaches		
Diarrhea		
Indigestion and stomach upset		
Ulcers		
Skin infections		
Eye infections		
Vaginitis		
Colds		
Pain relief		
Fever		
Nasal congestion		
Sinus pain		
Motion sickness		
Dehydration		
Insomnia		
Sun protection		
Insect protection		
Water purification		
Tooth fillings and inlays (temporary fillings)		
Eyeglasses (extra pair and repair kit)		
Bandages		
Sanitary products		
Condoms		

98

12 Tips to Keep Long-Distance Travel from Becoming Travail

Always remember that only two letters separate "travel" from "travail," so R-E-L-A-X and follow these 12 tips for a far more productive and enjoyable business trip.

1. Plan ahead. When flying across several time zones, adjust your bedtime a few days before your flight. Turn in later if going west—earlier if heading east.

2. Even before arriving at your destination, begin thinking on its time schedule in terms of what you do, drink, and eat.

3. Dress for comfort on your flight; wear loose-fitting clothes.

4. Take advantage of anything that can add to your travel comfort—neck pillows, eyeshades, earplugs, blankets—and remember that an exciting book can help pass the time very quickly. The bigger the print, the easier the book will be on the eyes!

5. Try to avoid heavy meals.

6. Drink lots of water, but skip alcohol and caffeine.

7. Stretch your legs with strolls up and down the aisle. Stretch the rest of your body with isometrics in your seat.

8. Use lubricating drops to combat tired, dry eyes.

9. When you arrive, *don't* plan a major meeting at a time when you would normally be asleep, especially if you need to be alert for a negotiating session.

10. Whenever you can, take daytime flights so you can arrive at your destination at bedtime.

11. Ideally, plan to arrive a day early and rest up before getting down to business.

12. Take along pictures of family and friends, your kid's latest drawing, and your favorite slippers. Though they take up space, these familiar items will help you keep oriented to your "home base."

Part X

The Tool Kit

Tool Kit: A set of materials needed to carry out your occupation.

That is what the nine charts in Part X are all about *and* you are officially authorized to duplicate them. That way, you'll never be at a loss for those many different forms—the assignment planners, working calendars, ledgers, graph sheets, flow charts, media analyzers, and marketing wheels—that you always needed but never had around.

99. Decisions and Actions
100. Working Calendar
101. Planning Ledger
102. Strategic Plotter
103. Flow Chart
104. Media Spending Analyzer
105. Customer Contact Planner
106. U.S. Market Planner
107. The Multi-Factor Marketing Wheel

Decisions and Actions

What	Who	When	✔

Working Calendar

Action	Sun.	Mon.	Tues.	Wed.	Thurs.	Fri.	Sat.

Planning Ledger

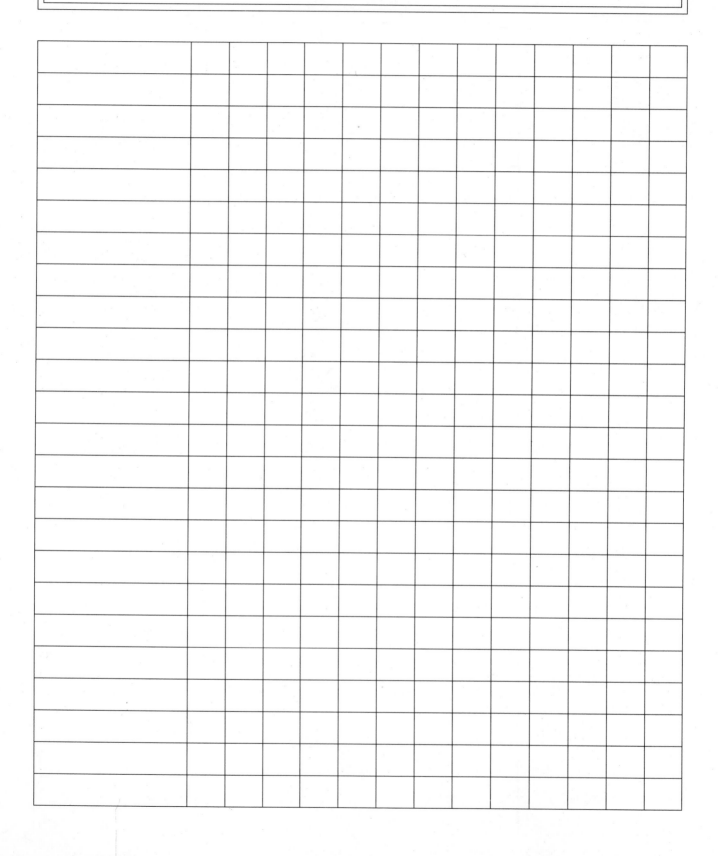

Strategic Plotter

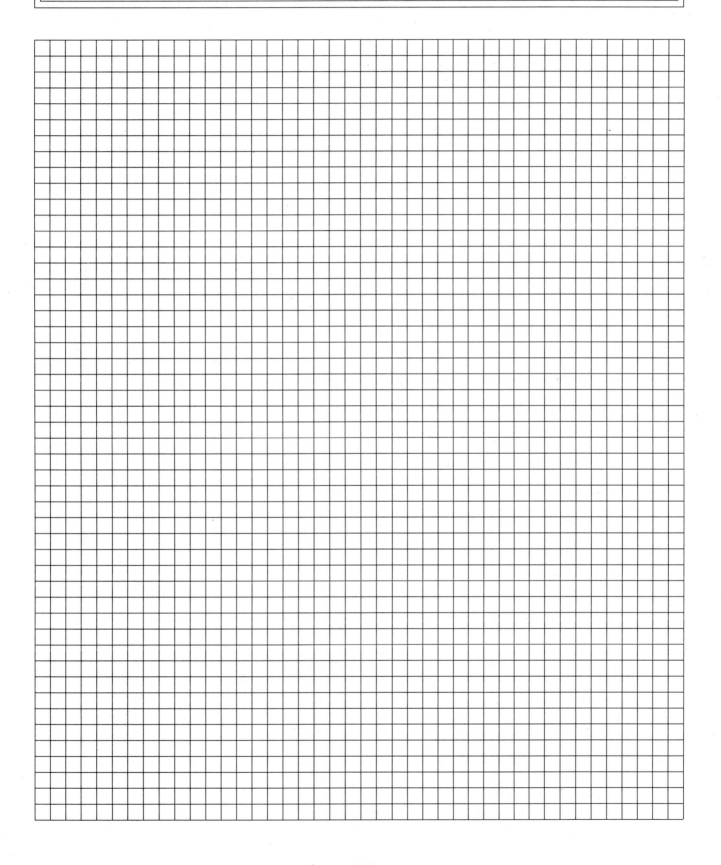

Flow Chart

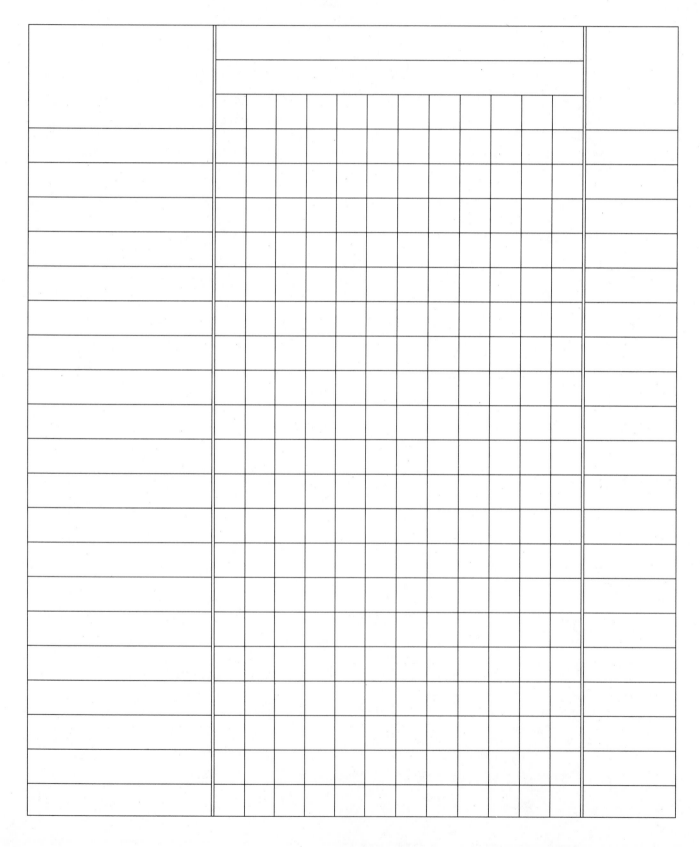

Media Spending Analyzer

Spending by Medium

Brand or Company	Magazines	Newspapers	Network TV	Spot TV	Network Radio	Spot Radio	Cable TV	Outdoor	Total $

Customer Contact Planner

Use the *Customer Contact Planner* to ensure that you consider not just the traditional media, but *all* options for reaching your prospects. These include seeing a movie, wheeling a shopping cart, riding a bus, working out at the health club, etc.

First, think carefully about everything that goes on during a day in the life of the prospects for your product. Then, note on the planner *every* specific opportunity you have to contact them across the day and across the week. Better still, have a group of your actual prospects fill it in. The results will focus your attention on many contact opportunities you otherwise might never consider. (See also Checklist 34 *107 Customer Contact Points from A to Z.*)

CUSTOMER CONTACT PLANNER

	Monday	Tuesday	Wednesday	Thursday	Friday	Saturday	Sunday
Awake, etc.							
Breakfast							
Work, etc.							
Break							
Lunch							
Work, etc.							
Break							
Dinner							
Relax, etc.							
To bed, etc.							

106

U.S. Market Planner

TELEVISION HOUSEHOLDS						
DMA RANK	**DMA MARKET**	**'000**	**%**			
1	New York	6692	7.11			
2	Los Angeles	5006	5.32			
3	Chicago	3071	3.26			
4	Philadelphia	2661	2.83			
5	San Francisco-Oak-San Jose	2253	2.39			
6	Boston	2105	2.24			
7	Washington, DC	1855	1.97			
8	Dallas-Ft. Worth	1817	1.93			
9	Detroit	1735	1.84			
10	Houston	1511	1.60			
		28707	30.48			
11	Atlanta	1510	1.60			
12	Cleveland	1447	1.54			
13	Seattle-Tacoma	1428	1.52			
14	Minneapolis-St. Paul	1389	1.48			
15	Tampa-St. Petersburg	1384	1.47			
16	Miami-Ft. Lauderdale	1297	1.38			
17	Pittsburgh	1142	1.21			
18	St. Louis	1109	1.18			
19	Sacramento-Stkton-Modesto	1100	1.17			
20	Phoenix	1097	1.17			
		12904	13.70			
21	Denver	1091	1.16			
22	Baltimore	970	1.03			
23	Orlando-Daytona Bch-Melbrn	967	1.03			
24	San Diego	921	0.98			
25	Hartford & New Haven	915	0.97			
26	Indianapolis	912	0.97			
27	Portland, OR	890	0.95			
28	Milwaukee	780	0.83			
29	Charlotte	775	0.82			
30	Cincinnati	770	0.82			
		8892	9.55			
31	Kansas City	768	0.82			
32	Raleigh-Durham	754	0.80			
33	Nashville	738	0.78			
34	Columbus, OH	711	0.75			
35	Greenvll-Spart-Ashevll-And	669	0.71			
36	Grand Rapids-Kalmzoo-B.Crk	639	0.68			
37	Buffalo	634	0.67			
38	Salt Lake City	617	0.65			
39	Norfolk-Portsmth-Newpt Nws	613	0.65			
40	San Antonio	611	0.65			
		6752	7.17			

Source: Nielsen Media Research (January 1994)

U.S. Market Planner

DMA RANK	DMA MARKET	'000	%			
	TELEVISION HOUSEHOLDS					
41	New Orleans	609	0.65			
42	Memphis	595	0.63			
43	Oklahoma City	572	0.61			
44	Harrisburg-Lncstr-Leb-York	570	0.61			
45	West Palm Beach-Ft. Pierce	566	0.60			
46	Providence-New Bedford	565	0.60			
47	Wilkes Barre-Scranton	550	0.58			
48	Greensboro-H.Point-W.Salem	538	0.57			
49	Louisville	533	0.57			
50	Albuquerque-Santa Fe	530	0.56			
		5629	5.98			
51	Birmingham	522	0.55			
52	Albany-Schenectady-Troy	509	0.54			
53	Dayton	509	0.54			
54	Jacksonville	484	0.51			
55	Richmond-Petersburg	484	0.51			
56	Charleston-Huntington	473	0.50			
57	Fresno-Visalia	473	0.50			
58	Little Rock-Pine Bluff	464	0.49			
59	Tulsa	456	0.48			
60	Flint-Saginaw-Bay City	448	0.48			
		4822	5.12			
61	Wichita-Hutchinson Plus	424	0.45			
62	Mobile-Pensacola	422	0.45			
63	Toledo	408	0.43			
64	Knoxville	404	0.43			
65	Green Bay-Appleton	392	0.42			
66	Roanoke-Lynchburg	386	0.41			
67	Syracuse	385	0.41			
68	Austin	383	0.41			
69	Lexington	379	0.40			
70	Honolulu	374	0.40			
		3957	4.20			
71	Rochester, NY	364	0.39			
72	Des Moines-Ames	363	0.38			
73	Omaha	360	0.38			
74	Shreveport	352	0.37			
75	Las Vegas	347	0.37			
76	Paducah-C.Gird-Harbg-Mt Vn	346	0.37			
77	Champaign & Springfld-Decatur	343	0.36			
78	Spokane	342	0.36			
79	Portland-Auburn, ME	341	0.36			
80	Springfield, MO	325	0.35			
		3481	3.70			

TELEVISION HOUSEHOLDS						
DMA RANK	DMA MARKET	'000	%			
81	Tucson (Nogales)	323	0.34			
82	Chattanooga	311	0.33			
83	Cedar Rapids-Waterloo & Dubq	301	0.32			
84	South Bend-Elkhart	299	0.32			
85	Ft. Myers-Naples	299	0.32			
86	Madison	298	0.32			
87	Huntsville-Decatur	297	0.32			
88	Davenport-R.Island-Moline	297	0.32			
89	Columbia, SC	296	0.31			
90	Jackson, MS	286	0.30			
		3006	3.19			
91	Johnstown-Altoona	284	0.30			
92	Burlington-Plattsburgh	283	0.30			
93	Tri-Cities, TN-VA	279	0.30			
94	Youngstown	275	0.29			
95	Evansville	269	0.29			
96	Baton Rouge	258	0.27			
97	Colorado Springs-Pueblo	251	0.27			
98	Waco-Temple-Bryan	248	0.26			
99	Springfield-Holyoke	247	0.26			
100	Lincoln & Hastings-Krny	245	0.26			
		2638	2.80			
101	El Paso	242	0.26			
102	Savannah	238	0.25			
103	Ft. Wayne	237	0.25			
104	Lansing	230	0.24			
105	Charleston, SC	230	0.24			
106	Greenville-N.Bern-Washngtn	229	0.24			
107	Sioux Falls (Mitchell)	220	0.23			
108	Fargo-Valley City	216	0.23			
109	Tyler-Longview (Lfkn & Ncgd)	214	0.23			
110	Santa Barbra-San Mar-San Lu Ob	212	0.22			
		2266	2.41			
111	Montgomery	211	0.22			
112	Augusta	208	0.22			
113	Peoria-Bloomington	208	0.22			
114	Monterey-Salinas	207	0.22			
115	Harlingen-Wslco-Brnsvl-Mca	203	0.22			
116	Tallahassee-Thomasville	199	0.21			
117	Eugene	199	0.21			
118	Ft. Smith	195	0.21			
119	Reno	195	0.21			
120	Lafayette, LA	195	0.21			
		2019	2.14			

TELEVISION HOUSEHOLDS						
DMA RANK	**DMA MARKET**	**'000**	**%**			
121	Traverse City-Cadillac	184	0.20			
122	Columbus, GA	182	0.19			
123	Yakima-Pasco-Rchlnd-Knnwck	180	0.19			
124	Macon	179	0.19			
125	Bakersfield	173	0.18			
126	Chico-Redding	173	0.18			
127	Florence-Myrtle Beach	170	0.18			
128	Duluth-Superior	170	0.18			
129	Corpus Christi	169	0.18			
130	Amarillo	169	0.18			
		1747	1.85			
131	Boise	168	0.18			
132	Monroe-El Dorado	167	0.18			
133	Wausau-Rhinelander	167	0.18			
134	Columbus-Tupelo-West Point	166	0.18			
135	La Crosse-Eau Claire	164	0.17			
136	Beaumont-Port Arthur	160	0.17			
137	Rockford	160	0.17			
138	Wheeling-Steubenville	158	0.17			
139	Wichita Falls & Lawton	152	0.16			
140	Wilmington	152	0.16			
		1612	1.71			
141	Erie	151	0.16			
142	Topeka	151	0.16			
143	Terre Haute	151	0.16			
144	Sioux City	151	0.16			
145	Medford-Klamath Falls	142	0.15			
146	Rochestr-Mason City-Austin	141	0.15			
147	Joplin-Pittsburg	139	0.15			
148	Binghamton	136	0.14			
149	Lubbock	135	0.14			
150	Bluefield-Beckly-Oak Hill	135	0.14			
		1430	1.52			
151	Columbia-Jefferson City	134	0.14			
152	Odessa-Midland	133	0.14			
153	Minot-Bismarck-Dickinson	131	0.14			
154	Albany, GA	129	0.14			
155	Bangor	124	0.13			
156	Anchorage	120	0.13			
157	Quincy-Hannibal-Keokuk	110	0.12			
158	Abilene-Sweetwater	107	0.11			
159	Biloxi-Gulfport	106	0.11			
160	Idaho Falls-Pocatello	104	0.11			
		1197	1.27			

| TELEVISION HOUSEHOLDS						
DMA RANK	DMA MARKET	'000	%			
161	Clarksburg-Weston	102	0.11			
162	Dothan	100	0.11			
163	Salisbury	98	0.10			
164	Utica	98	0.10			
165	Palm Springs	94	0.10			
166	Elmira	94	0.10			
167	Gainesville	92	0.10			
168	Hattiesburg-Laurel	90	0.10			
169	Panama City	89	0.09			
170	Watertown	87	0.09			
		944	1.00			
171	Alexandria, LA	87	0.09			
172	Billings	87	0.09			
173	Rapid City	85	0.09			
174	Missoula	77	0.08			
175	Greenwood-Greenville	76	0.08			
176	Jonesboro	75	0.08			
177	Lake Charles	75	0.08			
178	Yuma-El Centro	73	0.08			
179	Ada-Ardmore	70	0.07			
180	Great Falls	66	0.07			
		772	0.82			
181	Meridian	65	0.07			
182	Jackson, TN	62	0.07			
183	Parkersburg	60	0.06			
184	Grand Junction-Montrose	58	0.06			
185	St. Joseph	58	0.06			
186	Tuscaloosa	57	0.06			
187	Marquette	56	0.06			
188	Eureka	56	0.06			
189	Mankato	54	0.06			
190	Bowling Green	52	0.06			
		579	0.61			
191	Butte	50	0.05			
192	Cheyenne-Scottsbluf-Strlng	48	0.05			
193	Casper-Riverton	47	0.05			
194	Lafayette, IN	47	0.05			
195	San Angelo	46	0.05			
196	Charlottesville	44	0.05			
197	Anniston	43	0.05			
198	Ottumwa-Kirksville	41	0.04			
199	Laredo	40	0.04			
200	Lima	39	0.04			
		446	0.47			

	TELEVISION HOUSEHOLDS					
DMA RANK	DMA MARKET	'000	%			
201	Harrisonburg	38	0.04			
202	Bend, OR	33	0.03			
203	Twin Falls	32	0.03			
204	Zanesville	31	0.03			
205	Fairbanks	31	0.03			
206	Presque Isle	30	0.03			
207	Victoria	26	0.03			
208	Helena	20	0.02			
209	Alpena	16	0.02			
210	North Platte	15	0.02			
		272	0.29			
211	Glendive	4	0.00			
	Total U.S.	94176	100.00			

The Multi-Factor
Marketing Wheel

One of the most effective ways to visually demonstrate how various factors are related or impact upon an event is to show them as spokes on a wheel. *The Multi-Factor Marketing Wheel* may be used for this purpose.

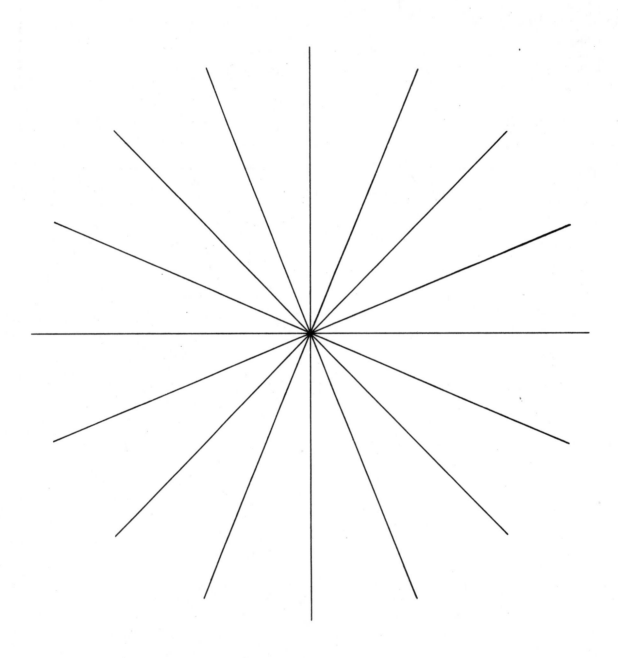